Copycat Recipes

Updated, Delicious, Quick, Healthy, and Easy to Follow Copycat Cookbook For Making Your Favorite Restaurant and Most Popular Dishes At Home The Ketogenic Way!

Dr I. Pot

COPYRIGHT

Table of Contents

INTRODUCTION

There's a proliferation of books, both printed and electronic (downloadable from the Web), that imply to reveal to you how to duplicate your preferred dishes from your preferred eateries. A portion of these are superior to other people, yet they all bring up the issue: Is it legitimate to "copycat" recipes along these lines?

Nowadays, with the music business following individuals who use record sharing administrations to illicitly present tunes for others on duplicate, and with conspicuous enemy of replicating alerts from the FBI stuck on each film DVD we lease or buy, it's a characteristic inquiry. Individuals wonder if they are violating some law by cloning a café's most well-known recipe- - regardless of whether it's by going around the guidelines or by really cooking and serving it to companions.

Brain you, I'm no attorney. Be that as it may, I've conversed with two or three legal counselor companions just as to various café administrators. The main concern is this: If you concoct your preferred steak or lobster dish (or whatever) replicated from Big Name Restaurant- - regardless of whether it's a careful copy - you need not stress that a SWAT group is going to separate your entryway and take you away. Nor will a multitude of legal advisors be plummeting on your kitchen.

Presently, if you choose to open your own café with dishes replicated from notable chain eateries, and if you are so un-unpretentious as to give them indistinguishable names from the firsts, you may experience difficulty on your hands! Shy of this improbable situation, you're most likely sheltered. Yet, we're not speaking here about starting a new business with others' recipes, right? (If you're mulling over anything along that line, then you truly should counsel a lawyer.)

Cooking for companions can be enjoyable. It very well may be increasingly fun if you serve them dishes that are actually similar to ones from their preferred café. If that is your goal, and you're doing it in a private setting, you can make your brain feel relaxed about the law. The main inquiry then becomes, what dish would I like to clone, and where would I be able to get a real recipe?

COPYCAT RESTAURANT FAVORITES: A GUIDE AND COMPILATION OF THE MOST

Here is my own rundown of my preferred copycat recipes for 2019. Throughout the years individuals ask me what are my preferred copycat recipes, and here is the rundown of my undisputed top choice recipes. This assortment is written arranged by eatery, presently the genuine blog contains a lot more recipes, yet here are my top choices.

Individuals solicit me all from the time what is my preferred recipe. I need to state pass on it is the Olive Garden Alfredo Sauce. For me, this was the recipe that kicked everything off.

Do copycat recipes truly pose a flavor like café recipes?

Copycat recipes can taste fundamentally the same as café recipes

Often café recipes are made with basic ingredients everybody can discover in their kitchen

You can copy a significant number of your preferred café dinners by reproducing the recipe at home

Some eatery recipes truly aren't extraordinary or made with mystery ingredients

A significant number of the most well-known eatery dishes are extremely exemplary dishes that we definitely know and love

Presently how we begin with the remainder of the recipes.

Applebee's

Applebees Grilled Chicken Oriental Salad

Applebees Queso Blanco

ARBYS

Arby's Sauce

Arby's Horsey Sauce

Barbecued Chicken and Pecan Salad

Huge BOY'S RESTAURANT

Strawberry Pie

BJ'S RESTAURANT AND BREWHOUSE

BJ's Restaurant and Brew house Pizzookie

Bison WILD WINGS

Bison Wild Wings

Bison Wild Wings Spicy Garlic Wings

BONEFISH GRILL

Sautéed Tilapia with Chimichurri Sauce

Bonefish Grill Bang Shrimp

BOSTON MARKET

Boston Market Sweet Potato Casserole

Boston Market Creamed Spinach

California Pizza Kitchen

California Pizza Kitchen Original BBQ Pizza

California Pizza Kitchen Chicken Tequila Fettuccine

Skipper D'S

Skipper D's Batter-Dipped Fish

Captain D's Cole Slaw

CARRABBAS

Carrabbas Sausage and Lentil Soup

Carrabbas Chicken Bryan

CHEDDAR'S

Cheddars Santa Spinach Dip Fe Dip

CHEESECAKE FACTORY

Cheesecake Factory Red Velvet Cheesecake

Cheesecake Factory Chicken Piccatta

Cheesecake Factory Oreo Cheesecake

CHIPOTLE MEXICAN GRILL

Chipotle Mexican Grill Guacamole

Chipotle Mexican Grill Cilantro Lime Rice

CHUY'S TEX MEX

Chuy's Tex Mex Creamy Jalapeno Dip

CHICKEN FIL A

Chick Fil A Chicken Nuggets

Chick Fil A Sauce

Copycat Chick Fil A Frosted Coffee

Chick Fil A Mac and Cheese

CHILI'S

Copycat Chilis Southwest Egg Rolls

COLD STONE CREAMERY CAKE BATTER ICE CREAM

Cold Stone Creamery Cake Batter Ice Cream

Wafer BARREL

Wafer Barrel Fried Apples

Wafer Barrel Grilled Chicken Tenders

Wafer Barrel Coca Cola Cake – another occasional forte that preferences simply like the genuine article.

Wafer Barrel Hashbrown Casserole

DAIRY QUEEN

Two Ingredients – Copycat Dairy Queen Oreo Blizzard

DUNKIN DONUTS

Dunkin Donuts Salted Caramel Hot Chocolate

Dunkin Donuts Coffee Coolatta

FRIENDLY'S

Agreeable's Peanut Butter Sauce

IHOP

IHOP Buttermilk Pancakes HOP Cinna-a-stack Pancakes

Here is my own rundown of my preferred copycat recipes for 2019. Throughout the years individuals ask me what are my preferred copycat recipes, and here is the rundown of my undisputed top choice recipes. This assortment is written arranged by eatery, presently the genuine blog contains a lot more recipes, however here are my top choices.

Individuals solicit me all from the time what is my preferred recipe. I need to state pass on it is the Olive Garden Alfredo Sauce. For me, this was the recipe that kicked everything off.

Do copycat recipes truly suggest a flavor like café recipes?

Copycat recipes can taste fundamentally the same as café recipes

Often eatery recipes are made with normal ingredients everybody can discover in their kitchen

You can copy huge numbers of your preferred café suppers by reproducing the recipe at home

Some eatery recipes truly aren't uncommon or made with mystery ingredients

A considerable lot of the most well-known café dishes are extremely exemplary dishes that we definitely know and love

MYSTERY RECIPES FOR BELOVED DISHES THAT RESTAURANTS ARE REVEALING

While a few of us are exploiting the way that a portion of our preferred cheap food and quick easygoing café networks are as yet offering drive-through, conveyance, and takeout, a large number of us have set aside this stay-at-home effort to cook more and eat out less often. If you need to keep on utilizing your cooking and heating muscles while enjoying your darling eatery suppers, there's currently a way you can have the best of the two universes.

From McDonald's to The Cheesecake Factory, the absolute most acclaimed café networks are revealing at-home forms of their well-known menu things— numerous unexpectedly.

What are you hanging tight for? Get in on the activity and get familiar with the insider facts behind a choice of the most well-known inexpensive food dishes ever. Peruse our rundown, set up a basic food item rundown of the ingredients you need, set out to find out about our 12 Best Tips for Safe Grocery Shopping Amid Coronavirus Concerns, and get to cooking.

Here are a couple of the mystery recipes eatery networks are imparting to you at this moment:

1   McDonald's Sausage and Egg McMuffin

We're totally serious. Toward the beginning of April, McDonald's UK posted the specific guidelines they follow to make one of the most famous inexpensive food breakfast things ever. The key to the ideal eggs? McDonald's adds a touch of water to the base of their griddle, heats it to the point of boiling, and afterward splits the eggs into ring mold. The technique basically poaches the eggs more than it fries them, bringing about the completely cooked egg round. If you found a container of eggs at the rear of your cooler to utilize and don't recollect when you got them, utilize our stunt for The Quickest Way to Tell If Eggs Are Still Good.

Get the recipe for McDonald's Sausage and Egg McMuffin

2   Burger King's Whopper

There are no guidelines or anything, yet Burger King France presented an info graphic on their Twitter account posting all the ingredients you'd have to assemble your own special Whopper at home.

Get the recipe for Burger King's Whopper

3   Chipotle's Guac Recipe

We needed to do a touch of burrowing for this one, however we recollected that Chipotle shared their Guac recipe with the world in 2015. Because the organization brought the recipe down, it is extremely unlikely to state without a doubt that these are as yet the proportions the Mexican easygoing café utilizes, however they were acceptable at one point in time, so we have no issue following this recipe to prepare a portion of the avocado fixing at home. On the off chance that the recipe vanishes once more, look at the ingredients here:

2 ready Hass avocados

1/4 cup red onion (finely hacked)

2 tsp lime juice

1/2 jalapeño, including seeds (finely slashed)

2 tbsp cilantro (cleaved)

1/4 tsp genuine salt

Get the recipe for Chipotle's Guac Recipe

4   Cheesecake Factory's Chinese Chicken Salad

When we heard the news that Cheesecake Factory was telling landowners that the cafés wouldn't have the option to pay April lease, we were profoundly, profoundly concerned. In any case, in the wake of raising a cool $200 million, we can feel comfort in knowing our valued super menu chain will in any case be around once social separating rules ease. Meanwhile, the Factory is holding us over by sharing 19 home-style forms of their most mainstream dishes. No, there's no cheesecake (you'll need to make do with our Copycat Cheesecake Factory recipe for that), and indeed, it's only a small amount of the 250 dishes the café network offers, however they're probably the best.

BREAKFAST

Regardless of whether you long for breakfast in bed or you're wanting breakfast for supper, these morning meal copycat dishes make certain to fill your day with daylight.

IHOP's Blueberry Pancakes

My father makes blueberry flapjacks for us each Saturday as a general rule. The blend of oats, cornmeal and buttermilk in the player gives the flapjacks healthiness we can't help it. — Gabrielle Short, Pleasant Hill, Iowa

Starbucks' Blueberry Muffin

My Aunt Betty is a significant pastry specialist, yet I anticipate these delicious blueberry biscuit recipe the most. She gives me enough with the goal that I can freeze and appreciate them for quite a long time. — Sheila Raleigh, Kechi, Kansas

Sway Evans' Biscuits and Gravy

This is an old Southern bread rolls and sauce recipe that I've adjusted. Hand crafted wiener sauce is a work of art, generous breakfast that takes you out traveling toward the South every time it's served. — Sue Baker, Jonesboro, Arkansas

Spread and Jelly Milk Shake at Home

Waffle House's Waffles

It was on a visit to my significant other's family members in Europe that I was given this Belgian waffle recipe. These hand crafted waffles are extraordinary with any sort of garnish: blueberries, strawberries, raspberries, seared apples, powdered sugar or whipped besting. — Rose Delemeester, St. Charles, Michigan

Panera's Four Cheese Soufflé

Regardless of when I've made these soufflés, they have consistently been a triumph. In spite of the fact that I've never observed the focuses begin to fall, it's ideal to anticipate serving them hot from the stove. — Jean Ference, Sherwood Park, Alberta

Bounce Evans' Country Fried Steak

As a kid, my grandma showed me how to make this breaded and fried steak. I showed my girls, and when my granddaughters are greater, I'll show them, as well. — Donna Cater, Fort Ann, New York

Dunkin Donut's Chocolate Glazed Donut

I originally attempted these delectable treats at my sister's home and thought they were the best I'd at any point had. They're anything but difficult to make, and the fudge icing finishes them off well. When I make them for companions, the recipe is constantly mentioned.

Mimi's Cafe's Eggs Benedict

Legend has it that poached eggs on an English biscuit began at Delmonico's in New York. Here's my interpretation of this informal breakfast great, and don't extra the hollandaise. — Barbara Pletzke, Herndon, Virginia

Saltine Barrel's Buttermilk Pancakes

You can't thump the best buttermilk hotcake recipe for a down-home generous breakfast. Pair it with wiener and new natural product for a scrumptious morning dinner. — Betty Abrey, Imperial, Saskatchewan

Dennys' Ham and Cheese Omelet

This simple omelet will be a no brainer to fix for breakfast or supper. — Agnes Ward, Stratford, Ontario

Cocos' Santa Fe Quiche

I found this quiche recipe numerous years prior, it's as yet one of my top picks today. It's speedy and simple, yet extremely delectable. It's additionally a decent dish to take to potlucks or fill in as a starter. You may like it for an informal breakfast or light dinner, as well. — Hazel Turner, Houston, Texas

Perkins Restaurant and Bakery's Maple Glazed Pork Chops and Eggs

Everybody cleaned their plates when my mom made this delicious, tart sweet pork cleaves when I was growing up. Presently I get similar outcomes when I serve them to my family close by fruit purée and au gratin potatoes. — Cheryl Miller, Fort Collins, Colorado

IHOP's Strawberry and Cream Crepes

I generally feel like a French gourmet expert when I serve these pretty crepes. In spite of the fact that they set aside a little effort to get ready, they're certainly justified regardless of the exertion. My visitors are constantly dazzled. — Debra Latta, Port Matilda, Pennsylvania

Dunkin Donut's Jelly Donut

There's no compelling reason to rush to the bread shop for flavorful jam doughnuts! These sweet treats are lighter than air. I've been fixing them for a long time for my significant other, our two little girls and their families. They vanish nearly as quickly as I make them. — Kathy Westendorf, Westgate, Iowa

McDonald's Hash Browns

Potato hotcakes, or latkes, are extremely flexible. Fresh outwardly and delicate within, they can be a side dish for pretty much any supper or the fundamental course for a quick bite. We have them often at our home. — Lydia Robotewskyj, Franklin, Wisco.

Cracker Barrel's French Toast with Fruit Sweet Topping

The wipe like nature of French toast gives it that "uncommon event" feel, however why keep it down when it's probably the simplest approaches to get egg and bread together in the first part of the day? Ready and waiting with a tart blueberry sauce. — Debbie Johnson, Centertown, Missouri

Town Inn's Ultimate Skillet

I found the recipe for this healthy burner dish quite a while back and transformed it to accommodate our preferences. When I served it at a Christmas early lunch, it was a moment hit. — Marilyn Hash, Enumclaw, Washington

Dennys' Loaded Veggie Omelet

New green pepper, onion and tomato give these appetizing omelet garden-new flavors. You can without much of a stretch fluctuate it dependent on the new ingredients you have close by. — Agnes Ward, Stratford, Ontario

McDonald's Egg McMuffin

I transformed exemplary breakfast sandwiches into something heartier you could have for supper, as well. We heap ingredients like salsa, avocado—even mayo and ketchup—onto my natively constructed bread rolls. — Fay Moreland, Wichita Falls, Texas

Burger King's French Toast Sticks

Figure out how to make French toast sticks with this fast and simple recipe. I like to have them helpful in the cooler for a healthy breakfast in a moment. They're extraordinary for buffets because they can be eaten in a hurry. — Taste of Home Test Kitchen, Milwaukee, Wisconsin

Starbucks' Orange Mango Smoothie

Treat yourself to this yummy mix of mango, pineapple, banana and nectar. The yogurt makes it rich and smooth, however a serving has just 2 grams of fat! — Taste of Home Test Kitchen

First Watch's Avocado Toast

This is such a simple method to add avocados to your eating regimen. Utilize sound multigrain bread and top with cut radishes and split pepper or lime get-up-and-go, or chipotle peppers and cilantro for additional flavor. You'll need to make this avocado toast recipe each morning! — Taste of Home Test Kitchen, Milwaukee, Wisconsin

Panera's Ham and Cheese Soufflé

I like to serve this scrumptious dish for informal breakfast alongside new organic product when I'm having visitors. In addition to the fact that it is simple, everybody appreciates it. Make it the prior night, then the following day you should simply heat it. — Airy Murray, Williamsport, Maryland

Waffle House's Pecan Waffles

I've pursued for a considerable length of time to copy a delightful waffle I ate at an eatery network here in the South. This is the nearest I've come, and they're fresh and nutty. Margarine and maple syrup are my family's preferred garnishes. Why not serve them for your vacation informal breakfast?

Chick-Fil-A's Hash Brown Scramble Burrito

I found breakfast burritos at a workshop of occasion morning meals offered at our congregation. It was a success! It works truly well when you're cooking for a group. I like to serve salsa or hot sauce with them. — Catherine Allan, Twin Falls, Idaho.

These genuine eatery Breakfast Recipes will kick your vacation day off right!

These most loved breakfast eatery recipes go from healthy, full-family charge to "get-it-and-go." All are heavenly, and nutritious. In any case, numerous things can be rapidly and effortlessly made early and served the following day ...or a few days after ...without lost quality!

You've presumably "surfed" onto this site needing or requiring some demonstrated breakfast recipes. That is extraordinary because you've discovered them!

This site has incredible café recipes. If you need the recipes in digital book structure or in a beautiful shading soft cover book, simply click here.

(Ruth is taking out ham and eggs with cabin singed potatoes and a side of rolls and wiener sauce. Somebody's eager!)

Every one of these recipes is eatery client tried and client endorsed. They work!

Most loved Breakfast Recipes

Fried Eggs For Buffet Service

Have a gathering wanting breakfast or early lunch and need to serve fried eggs? Here is the means by which to cook and hold the eggs so they are as yet hot and scrumptious when dishing up. Planning time: 10 minutes. Serves 6.

Fried Eggs With Smoked Wild Salmon

Recollections are holding on to be made with this fried egg recipe utilizing smoked wild salmon. I am lucky to live in Washington State (USA) because of the assortment of value items accessible. This is a simple eatery breakfast recipe however the "key" is utilizing quality smoked salmon. Planning time: 5 minutes. Serves 4.

Denver Omelet

This is truly outstanding and most popular American omelet. If it is mixed and set between cuts of toast it turns into a Denver sandwich and is similarly as acceptable. Planning Time: 8 minutes. Servings: 2.

Bacon, Spinach and Swiss Cheese Omelet

The mix of ingredients in this Bacon-Spinach-Swiss Omelet is extremely astounding. This egg recipe is an extraordinary method to begin your day! Planning time: 10 minutes. Serves 2

"I Never Sausage A Thing" Omelet

I like to have a great time naming a portion of my eatery recipes! This is a recipe for a flavorful wiener omelet. Planning time: 12 minutes. Serves 1-2.

Prepared Sausage And Cheese Omelet

Ring that morning meal chime! This prepared frankfurter omelet isn't just delightful and simple to cook, it is an entirely adaptable recipe. Planning time: 15 minutes. Serves 6-8

Low Fat Chicken Omelet

This tasty omelet is a low fat chicken omelet basically because the omelet is made distinctly with egg whites (no yolks). Planning time: 10 minutes. Servings: 1-2.

Shrimp Avocado Omelet

A gigantic selling omelet at my eatery when I run it as an extraordinary. The eatery recipe calls for sound shrimp with new avocado. Planning time: 8 minutes. Serves 1-2.

Wiener and Cheese Strata

Make this recipe early. Serve the following day when you think you'll be in a hurry. Incredible eatery style breakfast recipe and smorgasbord thing! Planning time: About 40 minutes. Recipe serves 12.

Nursery Frittata

A straight from-the-garden eatery frittata recipe makes a really delightful and nutritious supper. It is superb to live in a cultivating valley and have simple access to newly developed, hand-picked, natural vegetables and herbs. I utilize this gift with this recipe. Planning time: 25 minutes. Serves 4.

Italian Frittata

Brilliantly tasty blend of Italian frankfurter, a touch of garlic, marinara or Italian meat sauce and cheddar. Planning time: 12 minutes. Serves 2-4 individuals.

Corned Beef Hash

Corned Beef Hash is as much valued by my eatery visitors for breakfast just like a supper of Corned Beef and Cabbage. Planning time: 10 minutes. Serves 4.

Grain Muffins

One of the most mentioned breakfast recipes by papers just as clients (visitors). There IS a mystery to this eatery recipe. If refrigerated, the player will keep 5 weeks (cool!) Preparation Time: Approximately 20 minutes. This morning meal recipe will bring about 12-16 biscuits relying upon your container.

Blueberry Muffins

YUMMY! New or solidified berries. In a sharp cream hitter, these flavorful biscuits may turn into your Sunday morning luxury! Planning time: around 20 minutes. 16-20 servings.

Granola

Make this morning meal recipe ahead and in "mass." Serve with one of my "fab" biscuits; juice, espresso or tea. You have a scrumptious, nutritious, quick breakfast! Planning time: around 20 minutes. 10-12 servings.

Fall Harvest Quiche

An unordinary yet flavorful rustles quiche utilizing a large portion of an oak seed squash with eggs, pork frankfurter, apples and onions. Planning time: 25 minutes. Serves 6.

Truly, genuine men do eat quiche and bunches of it. This café recipe is a most loved with bacon and Swiss cheddar. Planning time: roughly 25 minutes. Serves 4.

Chicken and Mushroom Quiche

A perfect breakfast reward for individuals who couldn't care less for the more customary breakfast meats, for example, bacon, frankfurter or ham. Planning time: 30 minutes: Serves 4.

Wild Smoked Salmon Quiche

This eatery recipe for Smoked Salmon Quiche I as a rule include on a Sunday exceptional sheet. A Best Restaurant Breakfast Recipe. Planning time: 25 minutes. Serves 4.

Bacon (or Ham) and Spinach Frittata

In all honesty, I acquainted my clients with this morning meal various years back. This recipe currently sells like "hotcakes." My clients likewise like this frittata recipe for lunch and supper. Planning time: 15 minutes. Recipes serves 2.

"All Hams On Deck"

A delectable ham scramble with diced red potatoes, green pepper and red onions, all bested with my brilliant Hollandaise sauce. Planning time: 8 minutes. Serves 1-2 individuals.

"Popeye Scramble"

Obviously ...the title is because of the spinach and my eatery visitors and I named it what we accomplished for the sake of entertainment (once more). Planning time: 8 minutes. Serves 2 individuals.

Potato Scramble Recipe

We run this on our café exceptional sheet when we have extra cooked potatoes and I call it "grub." It sells well indeed. I have one other recipe I call "town grub" and it, as well, sells out. Individuals appear to identify with the term, yet the fact of the matter is ...they love this café breakfast recipe. So will you. Planning time is around 15 minutes. Serves 2. Appreciate!

Pan fried food Shrimp Scrambled Eggs

A mix of sound shrimp, red cabbage, bok choy, carrots and pea pods make this a strange, however flavorful, scramble. Planning time: 10 minutes. Serves 1-2.

Tuscan Chicken Scramble

I call this tasty chicken fried egg recipe a "Tuscan Chicken Scramble" basically because it contains spinach, basil, tomatoes, garlic and Mozzarella cheddar. Planning time: 10 minutes. Serves 1-2.

Wiener or Bacon or Ham Breakfast Sandwich

OK ...I let it be known. I built up my forms of a morning meal sandwich after the "brilliant curves" presented them. Be that as it may, my sandwiches are vastly improved tasting and increasingly nutritious. Planning time: 8 minutes. Serves 4.

Frittata Milanese

We previously made this genuine café frittata recipe for a gathering informal breakfast at the eatery. This frittata recipe was a hit!

Sourdough Breakfast Sandwich

This morning meal recipe is for a sourdough sandwich with fried eggs, peppers and mushrooms. You may include a meat decision if wanted, yet the sandwich is scrumptious and nutritious with no meat. Planning time: 8 minutes. Serves 1.

Breakfast Burrito with Eggs, Sausage, Potatoes and Cheese

These equivalent elements for this morning meal recipe can be utilized to cook a scramble yet I appreciate enveloping them all with a warm tortilla and having

salsa and guacamole served as an afterthought.
Planning Time: 20 minutes. Servings: 1-2.

Breakfast Burrito with Eggs and Potatoes and Green Chilies

No meat required for this café breakfast recipe! This scrumptious breakfast sandwich recipe came to me because of the impact of the Southwest and Mexico. Planning time: 10 minutes. Serves 1.

Buttermilk Pancakes

Goodness ...yummy! Scrumptious, wet and delicate and totally fantastic with a quality maple syrup or natural product beating. Planning time: 5-10 minutes. Serves: 6 enormous hotcakes.

Entire Wheat Blueberry Pancakes

The key to this "work of art" breakfast recipe is the player. Planning time: 15 minutes. 6-8 servings.

French Toast

This is a simple French Toast Recipe that my stupendous little girl eats each time she visits me at the café. Be that as it may, she isn't the only one. This French Toast "sells quickly!" Preparation time: 30 minutes. Serves: 4 or 16, 2 cuts each.

French Toast With Strawberry Butter

Most loved Restaurant Recipe With Children ...and I likewise discovered a great deal of grown-ups like this

French Toast Recipe with Strawberry Butter, as well. Planning time: 45 minutes. Makes 20 servings yet the recipe is anything but difficult to downsize.

Down-Home Sausage Gravy with Home-Made Buttermilk Biscuits

A recipe "two-fer." Make both. Pour the hot sauce over the scones for a treat you won't before long overlook! Planning time: around 25 minutes. 12 servings.

SECRET RESTAURANT COPYCAT RECIPES

Bean stew's Grilled Chicken Fettuccine

This copycat pasta recipe is rich and smooth, with a spike of Cajun flavoring. You won't have the option to accept this isn't from Chili's!

Serves: 2

Ingredients

- 2 boneless skinless chicken bosom parts, cut into strips

- 2 teaspoon Cajun flavoring

- 2 tablespoon spread or margarine

- 1 1/2 cup overwhelming cream

- 1/4 teaspoon dried basil

- 1/4 teaspoon lemon pepper flavoring

- 1/4 teaspoon salt

- 1/8 teaspoon pepper

- 1/8 teaspoon garlic powder

- 4 ounce fettuccine, cooked and depleted

- units of something

Directions

1.   Place chicken and Cajun flavoring in a bowl or resalable plastic sack; hurl or shake to cover.

2.   In a huge skillet over medium warmth, sauté chicken in margarine until practically delicate, around 5 to 7 minutes. Lessen heat. Include cream and flavoring; heat through. Include pasta and hurl; heat all through. Sprinkle Parmesan cheddar if wanted.

Macaroni Grill Focaccia

This rosemary focaccia is the ideal bread to plunge in a delightful olive oil. Serve this as a starter or use as the base for a healthy sandwich.

Serves: 8

Ingredients

* 9 tablespoon olive oil

* 3 cup universally handy flour, unsifted

* 3/4 cup semolina flour, unsifted

* 1/2 teaspoon salt

* 1 1/2 tablespoon brisk rising dry yeast

* 1 1/2 cup hot milk

* 1 tablespoon new rosemary leaves

Guidelines

1. Pour a sparse tablespoon of the olive oil into a 9-inch square cake skillet; spread uniformly to cover base and sides. Spot generally useful flour, semolina flour, 2 tablespoons of the olive oil, 1/4 teaspoon of the salt and the entirety of the yeast in the bowl of a blender fitted with a mixture snare. (The blending should be possible by hand too.) Blend ingredients on medium speed. Decrease speed to low and gradually include hot milk. Raise the speed to medium and keep blending for 5 minutes (work around 8 to 10 minutes by hand).

2.   Sprinkle base of cake container with a little flour. Expel batter from bowl and spread out uniformly in dish. Spread with a towel and let rest for 30 minutes.

3.   Preheat broiler to 400 degrees F.

4.   Remove towel. Brush mixture with 1 to 2 tablespoons of the olive oil. Sprinkle top with extra salt and rosemary. Heat for 20 minutes.

5.   Remove from broiler and sprinkle with outstanding oil.

Macaroni Grill Penne Rustica

This café copycat pasta dish is stacked with flavor. Between the shrimp, chicken, pancetta and the velvety sauce, this isn't a dish you will before long overlook.

Serves: 6

Ingredients

- 2 teaspoon spread
- 2 teaspoon garlic, hacked
- 1 teaspoon Dijon mustard
- 1 teaspoon salt
- 1 teaspoon rosemary, hacked
- 1 cup Marsala wine
- 1/4 teaspoon cayenne pepper
- 8 cup overwhelming cream
- 1 ounce pancetta or bacon
- of something
- 18 shrimp, stripped and deveined
- 12 ounce flame broiled chicken bosom, cut
- 4 1/2 cup sauce (from recipe underneath)
- 48 ounce penne pasta, cooked
- 3 teaspoon pimento
- 6 ounce spread
- 1 teaspoon shallots, hacked

- 1 squeeze salt and pepper

- 1 cup Parmesan cheddar

- 1/2 teaspoon paprika

- 6 twigs new rosemary

Directions

Gratinata Sauce (The sauce utilizes the ingredients recorded from spread through overwhelming cream)

1. Sauté margarine, garlic, and rosemary until garlic starts to brown. Include Marsala wine and lessen by 33%. Include remaining ingredients and diminish by half of unique volume. Put in a safe spot.

Penne Rustica:

2. Sauté pancetta until starts to brown. Include margarine, shallots, and shrimp. Cook until shrimp are equitably pink yet at the same time translucent. Include chicken, salt, pepper, and blend completely. Include gratinata sauce and 1/2 cup of parmesan cheddar and stew until sauce thickens.

3. In an enormous bowl, join shrimp and chicken blend with precooked pasta. Spot this blend into single serving dishes or one enormous goulash dish. Top with outstanding cheddar and pimientos and sprinkle with paprika. Prepare at 475 degrees F for 10 to 15 minutes. Expel and enhancement with new rosemary branch.

Macaroni Grill Roasted Garlic Lemon Vinaigrette

This serving of mixed greens dressing consolidates simmered garlic and light lemon juice to make the ideal flavor for an Italian plate of mixed greens. Top your preferred greens or veggies with this eatery copycat dressing from Macaroni Grill.

Ingredients

- 1/4 cup red wine vinegar
- 3 tablespoon nectar
- 1/2 tablespoon salt
- 1/2 ounce broiled garlic
- 3/4 cup olive oil
- 1/2 lemon, squeezed

Directions

1. Place vinegar, nectar, salt and broiled garlic in a food processor. Puree until garlic is cleaved fine.

2. With the food processor despite everything running, include olive oil and lemon juice. Refrigerate until prepared to utilize.

Macaroni Grill Shrimp Portofino

This straightforward and delightful shrimp dish is immaculate over rice or pasta. Attempt this copycat recipe from the Macaroni Grill today around evening time and please the whole family.

Serves: 4

Ingredients

- 16 medium mushrooms
- 2 teaspoon garlic, hacked
- 1/2 cup spread, dissolved
- 16 huge shrimp, cleaned
- 1/2 teaspoon pepper
- 1/4 cup new lemon juice
- 1 container marinated artichoke hearts
- 4 cuts lemon
- 2 tablespoon parsley

Directions

1. Saute mushrooms and garlic in spread until practically delicate. Include shrimp and sauté until shrimp is cooked, around 3 minutes (don't overcook!). Include remaining ingredients with the exception of lemon and parsley and warmth through.

2. Serve over pasta or rice. Enhancement with lemon cuts and parsley.

Sizzler Sizzlin' Onion Stack Steak

This café copycat recipe is pressed with flavor. Two sorts of onions beat high on an ideal steak make for a delightful and filling dinner. You can serve this with your preferred side dish, however we suggest a hot prepared potato.

Serves: 1

Ingredients

- 8 ounce most loved steak
- 1 1/2 teaspoon steakhouse flavoring
- 1 ounce onion straws
- 3 ounce caramelized onions
- 2 twigs parsley
- Au jus

Directions

1. Prepare steak exactly as you would prefer utilizing your preferred steak house flavoring.
2. Place 3 ounces of caramelized onions on plate. When steak is prepared, place steak on caramelized onions. Top steak with Onion Straws. Sprinkle hacked parsley on Onion Straws.
3. Serve with heated potato or vegetable of your decision.

Taco Bell Meat Seasoning

If you love Taco Bell (and let's be honest - who doesn't?), you'll be so eager to make this copycat recipe for their meat flavoring. There's something extraordinary about the kind of a Taco Bell taco, and now you can reproduce it at home. Charm hoo!

Serves: 6

Cooking Time: 30 min

Ingredients

- 1 1/3 pound lean finely ground toss
- 1 1/2 tablespoon Mesa Corn Flour
- 4 1/2 teaspoon bean stew powder

- 1/2 teaspoon onion powder
- 1/2 teaspoon garlic powder
- 1/2 teaspoon prepared salt
- 1/2 teaspoon paprika
- 1/4 teaspoon cumin
- 1/2 teaspoon garlic salt
- 1/4 teaspoon sugar
- 1 teaspoon dry minced onions
- 1/2 teaspoon hamburger bouillon

Guidelines

1.	Mix together all fixing aside from the meat. Mix the flavor blend well creation sure that the sum total of what flavors have been mixed well.

2.	Crumble ground meat and earthy colored blending admirably.

3.	Remove from heat, wash with boiling water and channel water and oil from meat.

4.	Return ground throw to the skillet and include taco flavoring.

5.	Add 3/4 - 1 cup water to ground meat and taco flavoring and stew on medium low temperature for 20 minutes.

6.	Simmer until the greater part of dampness has cooked away.

7.	Remove from heat when dampness in meat as disseminated however meat isn't dry.

Taco Bell Chalupa Supreme

Taco Bell's food is known for being cheap, however why not set aside yourself considerably more cash by remaining at home and making a copycat recipe

Ingredients

*   1 pound ground meat
*   1/4 cup flour
*   1 tablespoon stew powder
*   1 teaspoon paprika
*   1 teaspoon salt
*   1 tablespoon dried minced onion
*   1/2 cup water
*   flat bread (pita will work)
*   oil (for profound broiling)
*   sour cream, to taste
*   shredded lettuce, to taste
*   shredded Cheddar/jack cheddar, to taste
*   diced tomatoes, to taste

Directions

1. Mix dried onion with water in a little bowl and let represent five minutes.

2. Combine ground meat, flour, bean stew powder, paprika and salt. Blend well. Include onions and water. Blend once more. In a skillet, cook meat blend until seared. Mix often while cooking so no enormous lumps structure; it ought to be progressively similar to a glue.

3. Remove from warmth and keep warm. In a profound fryer (or you can utilize a skillet) profound fry

the bread for 30 seconds. Let channel on permeable towels. Assemble Chalupas beginning with meat, then acrid cream, lettuce cheddar, and tomatoes in a specific order. Top with hot sauce or salsa if wanted.

Andiamo's Raspberry Chocolate Mini-Cakes

This sweet and refined copycat recipe originates from Andiamo, a famous California café. Ambivalent chocolate and raspberries give these little cakes gourmet taste.

Ingredients
- 1 container new raspberries
- 3/4 cup granulated sugar
- 1/4 cup liquor
- 1/4 teaspoon cinnamon
- 1 tablespoon unsweetened cocoa powder
- 2 ounce self-contradicting or semisweet chocolate, cleaved
- 1/4 cup unsalted margarine, cut little
- 2 enormous egg yolks
- 1 enormous egg
- of something

Guidelines

1. Combine raspberries with 1/2 cup sugar, liquor and cinnamon in a medium pan. Mix and stew over medium warmth until sugar breaks down and sauce thickens, around 10 minutes.

2. Remove 1/4 cup of raspberries from pan and channel, sparing sauce. Margarine two 3/4 cup custard

cups. Whisk cocoa and staying 1/4 cup sugar in a little bowl.

3.   Stir chocolate and margarine in substantial little pan over low warmth until chocolate melts and blend is smooth. Speed in cocoa blend. Rush in egg yolks, then entire egg and flour. Overlap in held 1/4 cup berries.

4.   Bake at 350 degrees F until edges are set and center is still shiny and tester comes out with some wet batter attached, about 22 minutes.

5.   To serve, cut around warm cakes to loosen. Turn out onto plates. Spoon sauce on the side. Sift confectioners' sugar over and garnish with mint.

Notes

Cakes are to have a slightly soft center. both sauce and cakes can be made ahead of time. Cakes can be made ahead of time and refrigerated. When ready to eat, heat in microwave for about 1 minute.

Applebee's Vegetable Pizza with Spinach-Artichoke Sauce

Copycat vegetable pizza uses delicious spinach-artichoke dip as a sauce, rather than tomatoes. It's not your typical pizza, but that's what makes it so interesting!

Ingredients

- 1 10 inch flour tortilla
- butter-flavor oil, as needed
- 1/2 cup sliced mushrooms
- black pepper, to taste
- granulated garlic, to taste
- salt, to taste
- 4 ounce Hot Spinach and Artichoke Dip
- 1/4 cup tomatoes, diced
- 1/2 teaspoon Italian seasoning
- 1/2 cup mozzarella cheese, shredded

Instructions

1. To make pizza: In a hot sauté pan or on a griddle, place sliced mushrooms and butter-flavor oil and season with salt, pepper and garlic. Cook until hot.

2. Brush tortilla with oil and place on griddle. Spread spinach and artichoke dip evenly on top of tortilla to within 1/2 inch of the edge. Top with mushrooms, when cooked, Italian seasoning and diced tomatoes. Sprinkle shredded mozzarella cheese over pizza and remove from griddle and place on a pizza pan in an oven preheated to 350 degrees F. Remove from oven when cheese is melted and top with shredded Parmesan/Romano cheese. Cut into wedges and serve.

TO MAKE SPINACH AND ARTICHOKE DIP:

1 (10 ounce) box frozen, chopped spinach, thawed

1 (14 ounce) can artichoke hearts, drained and rough chopped 1 cup shredded parmesan/Romano cheese blend

1/2 cup shredded mozzarella cheese 10 ounces prepared Alfredo sauce

1 teaspoon minced garlic

4 ounces (1/2 package) softened cream cheese

1.   Combine ingredients thoroughly in a bowl and spread mixture into a small baking dish. Bake in an oven preheated to 350 degrees F for 30 minutes or until cheeses are bubbling and melted. Serve as sauce for the pizza, or as dip for bread or chips.

Buca di Beppo-Style Chicken Marsala

Buca di Beppo has become hugely popular thanks to its family-sized servings of Italian favorites. Now you can cook up a big plate of restaurant-quality chicken marsala at home using this copycat restaurant recipe.

Ingredients

- olive oil, to taste

- 4 thin chicken breast cutlets

- 2 ounce low salt bacon, cut into 1/4 inch pieces

- 1/2 cup all purpose flour

- coarse salt

- freshly ground pepper, to taste

- 1/2 cup dry Marsala wine

- 3 tablespoon heavy cream

Instructions

1. Coat a large skillet lightly with olive o9il and set over medium-high heat. Add bacon and cook until crisp and lightly browned. Remove with a slotted spoon; set aside. Leave fat in pan. Put flour on a plate. Pat cutlets dry. Season lightly with salt and pepper, then dredge in flour.

2. Heat pan with bacon fat over medium-high heat. Add a touch more olive oil if necessary to make approximately 2 tablespoons. When fat is hot, shake

excess flour off cutlets and place in pan. Sauté, turning once until browned on both sides. Thin cutlets should only take a few minutes per side. Remove cutlets. Pour excess fat from pan. With pan over medium-high heat, add the Marsala and scrape up the browned bits from the bottom of the pan. Cook Marsala until it is reduced by one quarter.

3.   Stir in cream and simmer until you get a nicely thickened sauce. Return the chicken and bacon to the pan and turn the cutlets to coat and reheat for a minute. Serve with the sauce over the top, with a sprinkling of parsley.

Cheesecake Factory Bruschetta

This is one of the most delicious recipes for one of the simplest appetizers - you can't go wrong. Serve copycat Cheesecake Factory Bruschetta at your next dinner party.

Ingredients

- 1 1/2 cup chopped Roma tomatoes
- 3 tablespoon diced red onions
- 1 large clove garlic, minced
- 2 tablespoon fresh basil, chopped
- 2 tablespoon olive oil
- 1/2 teaspoon red wine vinegar
- 1/4 teaspoon salt
- freshly ground black pepper, to taste
- 1/2 loaf French baguette or crusty Italian bread
- 3 sprigs cilantro

Instructions

1.　　Combine tomatoes, red onion, garlic and basil in a medium bowl. Add 1/2 tablespoon of oil, vinegar, salt and pepper and mix well. Cover the bowl and refrigerate for one hour.

2.　　When ready to serve, preheat broiler and slice the baguette in 1-inch slices on a 45 degree angle to make 5 to 7 slices of bread.

3.　　Combine remaining 1 1/2 tablespoons oil with the garlic salt. Brush entire surface of both sides of each slice with olive oil mixture. Broil slices for 1 1/2 to 2 minutes per side, until surface

starts to brown. Arrange bread like wheel spokes on serving plate. Spoon the chilled tomato in neatly onto bread slices where they meet at the center of the plate. Garnish with cilantro.

Copeland's of New Orleans Beer Cheese Ball

This delicious appetizer is packed with cheesy flavor and has a hint of beer. Serve this restaurant copycat recipe with your favorite bread or crackers. It's sure to be a hit.

Ingredients

- 1 pound cheddar cheese, grated
- 1 pound Velveeta cheese, grated
- 3 cloves garlic, chopped
- 3 tablespoon Worcestershire sauce
- 1/2 can beer
- 1 teaspoon salt
- 1 teaspoon powdered mustard
- Tabasco sauce, to taste
- Paprika, for garnish
- Parsley, chopped, for garnish

Instructions

1. Combine ingredients; shape into desired form. Wrap cheese with plastic wrap; refrigerate overnight.
2. Unwrap cheese; sprinkle with paprika and parsley.
3. Serve with crackers.

Jimmy Buffet's Margaritaville Cheeseburger in Paradise

There's nothing like a restaurant-quality burger in the comfort of your own home. Try this copycat recipe from Jimmy Buffet's Margaritaville and you'll never make another burger again.

Yields: 4

Ingredients

*   28 ounce USDA choice beef chuck, diced
*   2 tablespoon Kosher salt
*   1 tablespoon ground black pepper
*   1/2 teaspoon garlic salt
*   1/2 teaspoon onion salt
*   1 teaspoon celery salt
*   8 slices American cheese
*   4 sesame hamburger buns, toasted
*   8 leaves iceberg lettuce
*   4 slices tomato, .25 inch thick
*   4 slices red onion, .25 inch thick
*   4 toothpicks
*   4 pickle spears
*   2 pound Idaho potatoes, peeled, cut into fries and fried golden brown

Instructions

1.   Using a meat grinder with a 3/8-inch plate, grind the meat. Change to a 1/8-inch plate, and grind a second time. Shape the ground meat into 4 (7-ounce) patties.

2.   In a mixing bowl, combine the kosher salt, pepper, garlic salt, onion salt and celery salt. Mix well.

3.   Place burger on a hot grill and season with the seasoning salt. Cook the burgers halfway to desired temperature and flip over and finish cooking.

4.   Place cheese on the burger when it is 3/4 of the way cooked and melt. Place bottom bun on plate. Place burger on bottom bun. Place lettuce, tomato and onion on top of the burger. Cover with top bun and secure with a wooden pick. Place pickle next to the burger. Place fries on the plate.

T.G.I. Friday's Lemon Chicken with Pasta

Use this copycat recipe to make a delicious take on Chicken Scaloppini. Lemon Chicken with Pasta is a delicious melding of savory and zesty flavors.

Ingredients

- 2 1/2 pound chicken breasts (pounded thin)
- 2 ounce olive oil
- 8 ounce sliced mushrooms
- 2 lemons, halved
- 4 ounce heavy whipping cream
- 4 artichokes
- 4 teaspoon parsley
- 12 ounce lemon sauce
- 20 ounce angel hair pasta
- 8 tablespoon fried pancetta
- 1 tablespoon fresh lemon juice
- 4 tablespoon fried capers
- 1 quart Chablis
- 3 teaspoon butter
- 1 quart whipping cream
- 1 tablespoon thyme
- salt and pepper, to taste

Instructions

1.   For Chicken: Heat sauté pan to medium heat. Add oil and heat. Add chicken pieces to sauté pan and sauté on each side for one minute (or until no longer pink). Add sliced mushrooms to sauté pan and sauté with chicken for an additional minute. When mushrooms are cooked, squeeze juice from lemons into sauté pan and

coat the chicken with juice (ensure there are no seeds). Add cream to pan and stir to incorporate. Bring to a boil. Cut artichoke halves in half

again lengthwise, add to pan and cook for 15 seconds. Remove pan from heat. Add parsley and stir to incorporate. Add lemon sauce and stir to incorporate. DO NOT RETURN PAN TO HEAT/FLAME.

2.   For Sauce: Boil Chablis to reduce to 2 cups. Add lemon juice, butter and melt slowly. Add whipping cream and simmer on low heat until thickened. Add spices and cool to room temperatures.

3.   In large bowl, twirl pasta into a nest. Sprinkle chicken pieces against pasta and pour remaining contents of pan on and around the chicken. Sprinkle pancetta and capers over the entire dish. Garnish with chopped parsley.

Weber Grill's Famous Sangria

Sangria is a type of wine punch common to the Iberian Peninsula, but it's very popular right here in the USA as well. This version copies the delicious sangria made at the Weber Grill, and it is just as tasty!

Ingredients
*   1 Granny Smith apple, diced
*   1 Red Delicious apple, diced
*   1 Bartlett pear, diced
*   1 orange, sliced
*   2 limes, sliced

- 1 cup simple syrup (equal amounts sugar and water heated until sugar is dissolved)
- 3/4 pint orange juice
- 3/4 cup brandy
- 3/4 cup Triple Sec

Instructions

1. Combine all ingredients and gently mix.
2. Place in a container and refrigerate.
3. Serve base with equal parts sparkling wine or Champagne.

Wendy's Chili

As restaurant copycat recipes go, this version of Wendy's Chili is bang-on! We swear, if you put it into one of those paper cups like they serve it in at Wendy's, you'd be hard-pressed to tell this was simply a restaurant copycat recipe. It tastes just like Wendy's chili!

Serves: 8

Cooking Time: 3 hr

Ingredients

- 2 pound ground beef
- 1 29-ounce can tomato sauce
- 1 29-ounce can kidney beans with liquid
- 1 29-ounce can pinto beans with liquid
- 1 medium onion, diced
- 2 green chiles, diced
- 1 rib celery, diced
- 3 medium tomatoes, chopped
- 2 teaspoon cumin powder
- 3 tablespoon chili powder
- 1 1/2 teaspoon black pepper
- 2 teaspoon salt
- 2 cup water

Instructions
1.   Brown the beef and drain the fat off.
2.   Crumble the cooked beef into pea size pieces.
3.   In a large pot, combine the beef with the remaining ingredients and bring to a simmer over low heat.
4.   Cook, stirring every 15 minutes, for 2-3 hours.

T.G.I.   Friday's Garlic Chicken and Potatoes

A delicious dinner from T.G.I. Friday's - or is it? This chicken copycat recipe tastes so much like the real thing, you won't be able to tell it's home-made!

Ingredients

- 1/2 ounce garlic butter
- 2 chicken breasts, pounded and seasoned with garlic
- mixed vegetables
- mashed potatoes
- 1 tablespoon sliced green onion
- 2 tablespoon garlic chips
- of something

Instructions

1. Heat sauté pan over medium heat; add garlic butter and cook for 30 seconds. Place seasoned chicken breasts in pan and sauté on each side for 1&1/2 minutes.

2. While finishing the chicken, add the vegetables. Flash sauté vegetables to coat with marinade. Mound mashed potatoes in the center of service plate and garnish with green onions.

3. Remove chicken from sauté pan and shingle breasts slightly on mashed potatoes. Distribute vegetables with juices around mashed potatoes. Distribute fried garlic chips over chicken breasts. Garnish with chopped parsley.

P.F. Chang's Chicken Lettuce Wraps

This iconic dish became a copycat at many restaurants during the low-carb craze. Try this version from the restaurant that started it all. These chicken wraps are quick and easy and can be made as an appetizer or main course.

Serves: 1

Ingredients

- 8 dried shiitake mushrooms
- 1 teaspoon cornstarch
- 2 teaspoon dry sherry
- 2 teaspoon soy sauce
- 2 teaspoon water
- Salt and pepper
- 1 1/2 pound boneless skinless chicken breasts
- 5 tablespoon vegetable oil
- 1 teaspoon fresh ginger, minced
- 2 cloves garlic, minced
- 2 green onions, minced
- 2 small dried chiles (optional)
- 8 ounce can bamboo shoots, minced
- 8 ounce can water chestnuts, minced
- 1 package Chinese rice noodles, prepared according to package
- Iceberg lettuce leaves

Instructions

Cooking Sauce:

1 tablespoon Hoisin sauce 1 tablespoon soy sauce

1   tablespoon dry sherry

2   tablespoons oyster sauce 2 tablespoons water

1   teaspoon sesame oil 1 teaspoon sugar

2   teaspoons cornstarch

1.   Cover mushrooms with boiling water, let stand 30 minutes then drain. Cut and discard woody stems. Mince mushrooms. Set aside.

2.   Mix all ingredients for cooking sauce in bowl, and set aside.

3.   In medium bowl, combine cornstarch, sherry, soy sauce, water, salt, pepper and chicken. Stir to coat chicken thoroughly. Stir in 1 teaspoon oil and let sit 15 minutes to marinate. Heat wok or large skillet over medium high heat. Add 3 tablespoons oil, then add chicken and stir fry for about 3-4 minutes. Set aside.

4.   Add 2 tablespoons oil to pan. Add ginger, garlic, chiles (if desired), and onion; stir fry about a minute or so. Add mushrooms, bamboo shoots and water chestnuts; stir fry an additional 2 minutes. Return chicken to pan. Add mixed cooking sauce to pan. Cook until thickened and hot.

5.   Break cooked cellophane noodles into small pieces, and cover bottom of serving dish with them. Then pour chicken mixture on top of noodles. Spoon into lettuce leaf and roll.

P.F. Chang's Firecracker Shrimp

Spice up dinner with this copycat recipe from P.F. Chang's China Bistro. This dish is the perfect way to save on takeout and create an authentic Chinese dish on your own. Serve this with your favorite rice.

Serves: 2

Ingredients

- 2 tablespoon canola oil
- 8 ounce shrimp
- 7 baby carrots, halved lengthwise
- 1/2 cup water chestnut slices
- 24 snow peas
- 1 large scallion (white part), minced into .25 inch pieces
- 1 large garlic clove, chopped
- 2 tablespoon sherry
- 1 tablespoon sambal chili paste
- 1/4 teaspoon ground white pepper
- 2 teaspoon ground bean sauce
- Cilantro (for garnish)
- Cornstarch slurry (1 teaspoon cornstarch blended with 1 ounce water)

Instructions

Sauce:

2 tablespoons soy sauce

2 teaspoons granulated sugar 2 ounces water

2 teaspoons white vinegar

Assemble sauce ingredients and put aside.

1.   Heat a large sauté pan, cast iron skillet, or electric wok until smoking. Add oil and baby carrots, sauté until the color of carrots brightens.

2.   Add shrimp and stir fry until about halfway cooked. Add water chestnuts, snow peas and garlic. Sauté briefly. Add scallions. Add chili paste, ground white pepper, ground bean sauce, when you smell the "nuttiness" of the ground bean sauce, reduce heat and add sherry.

3.   Introduce sauce mixture, let boil briefly. Add cornstarch slurry and stir until thickened (approximately 30 seconds). Serve with steamed rice on platter or in large bowl, garnish with cilantro.

This Chinese chicken chow fun dish is the perfect dinner for two. Spend the night in instead of going to a crowded restaurant with this delicious copycat recipe from a popular Asian chain.

Serves: 2

Ingredients

•   4 ounce ground chicken, cooked
•   14 ounce chow fun noodles (wide rice noodles sold at most Asian markets)
•   2 tablespoon scallions, minced
•   1 teaspoon garlic, minced
•   1 teaspoon chili paste
•   1 teaspoon Szechuan preserved vegetables

- 2 tablespoon black fungus mushrooms, shredded

Instructions

Sauce:

2 tablespoons soy sauce 2 tablespoons vinegar

2 tablespoons granulated sugar 1 teaspoon oyster sauce

1 teaspoon mushroom soy sauce 2 tablespoons water

1. Separate the chow fun noodles and cover with plastic wrap until ready for service. Heat wok and add 2 teaspoons vegetable oil. Stir fry garlic and chill paste for 5 to 7 seconds. Add ground chicken sear with garlic and chill paste. Add black fungus mushrooms and sauce stir-fry briefly.

2. Separate the noodles and drop into the wok while you are mixing a handful at a time. Continue cooking until the noodles have absorbed all the flavors and are hot. Finish with sesame oil.

3. Serve into bowls or plates. Garnish with Szechwan preserved vegetables and minced scallions.

Arby's Copycat Horsey Sauce

This imitation recipe is mild but tangy, just like the original. Instead of going out, slather this copycat sauce on some roast beef for a taste just as delicious as the real thing!

Ingredients

- 1 cup mayonnaise
- 3 tablespoon bottled horseradish cream sauce
- 1 tablespoon granulated sugar

Instructions

1. Mix all ingredients together well. Keep refrigerated, tightly covered. Will keep up to 2 weeks.

Carrabba's Italian Grill Bread Dip Mix

This flavorful bread dip is packed with herbs and spices. Try this restaurant copycat recipe next time you have company. It's a quick and easy appetizer that will have everyone asking for seconds.

Ingredients

- 1 tablespoon crushed red pepper
- 1 tablespoon black pepper
- 1 tablespoon dried oregano
- 1 tablespoon dried rosemary
- 1 tablespoon dried basil
- 1 tablespoon dried parsley
- 1 tablespoon garlic powder
- 1 tablespoon garlic, minced
- 1 teaspoon salt

Instructions

1. Grind together.
2. To use, put 1 tablespoon of mixture in a small bowl. Pour extra virgin olive oil over and mix together. Dip warm sourdough French bread into the mixture.

Chili's Margarita Presidente

Create your own happy hour with this delicious version of Chili's famous margarita. Enjoy a bowl of tortilla chips and salsa with your margarita. You'll never want to leave the house again!

Ingredients

- 1 1/4 ounce Sauza Commemorativo Tequila
- 1/2 ounce Presidente brandy
- 1/2 ounce Cointreau
- 4 ounce sour mix
- Splash of lime juice
- of something

Instructions

1. Mix all ingredients together and serve in a salt rimmed Margarita glass filled with ice.

O'Charley's Loaded Potato Soup

Creamy cheesy potato soup is a restaurant favorite that can now be made at home with this great copycat recipe. This soup is hearty enough to be served as a meal.

Serves: 8

Cooking Time: 30 min

Ingredients

- 3 pound red potatoes
- 1/4 cup margarine
- 1/4 cup flour
- 8 cup half-and-half

- 16 ounce Velveeta cheese, melted
- White pepper, to taste
- Garlic powder, to taste
- 1 teaspoon hot pepper sauce
- 1/2 pound bacon, fried
- 1 cup cheddar cheese, shredded
- 1/2 cup fresh chives, chopped
- 1/2 cup fresh parsley, chopped

Instructions

1. Dice unpeeled red potatoes into 1/2-inch cubes. Place in a large Dutch oven, cover with water and bring to a boil. Let boil for 10 minutes or until 3/4 cooked.

2. In a separate large Dutch oven, combine melted margarine and flour, mixing until smooth. Place over low heat and gradually add half-and-half, stirring constantly.

Continue to stir until smooth and liquid begins to thicken.

3. Add melted Velveeta. Stir well. Drain potatoes and add to cream mixture. Stir in pepper, garlic powder and hot pepper sauce. Cover and cook over low heat for 30 minutes, stirring occasionally.

4. Place soup into individual serving bowls and top with crumbled bacon, shredded cheese, chives and parsley.

Nutritional Information

Per serving: 915 calories, 65 g fat (64 percent calories from fat), 174 mg cholesterol, 33 g protein, 52 g carbohydrate, 1,352 mg sodium

Cracker Barrel Old Country Store Cherry Chocolate Cobbler

Chocolate and cherry is a winning combination. Try them together in this delicious copycat version of Cracker Barrel's cherry chocolate cobbler. This is perfect served warm with whipped cream.

Serves: 6

Cooking Time: 45 min

Ingredients

- 1 1/2 cup all-purpose flour

- 1/2 cup granulated sugar

- 2 teaspoon baking powder

- 1/2 teaspoon salt

- 1/4 cup butter

- 6 ounce semisweet chocolate morsels

- 1/4 cup milk

- 1 egg

- 21 ounce can cherry pie filling

- 1/2 cup nuts, finely chopped

Instructions

1. Preheat oven to 350 degrees F.

2.   In large bowl, combine flour, sugar, baking powder, salt and butter; cut with pastry blender until crumbs are size of large peas. Melt over hot (not boiling) water, semisweet chocolate morsels. Remove from heat and cool slightly at room temperature (about 5 minutes). Add milk and egg to melted chocolate and mix well. Blend chocolate into flour mixture.

3.   Spread cherry pie filling in bottom of a 2-quart casserole. Drop chocolate batter randomly over cherries. Sprinkle with chopped nuts. Bake at 350 degrees F for 40 to 45 minutes.

Olive Garden Breadsticks

Everyone knows the breadsticks from the Olive Garden. Buttery, chock full of herbs and delicious. Make these at home to go perfectly with your next pasta dish or to serve alongside a beautiful salad.

Yields : 8
Preparation Time: 2 hr Cooking Time: 25 min
Ingredients
•   1 loaf of frozen bread dough, thawed and at room temperature
•   Pam spray
•   Garlic powder, to taste
•   Oregano, dried, to taste
Instructions
1.   When dough is soft enough to knead, spray your fingers with Pam or oil and knead just until you can shape into cigar-size pieces (about 8 to 10). Place these 3 inches apart on Pam-sprayed cookie sheets.
2.   Let rise in a warm place until doubled - about 1 1/2 to 2 hours.
3.   Holding Pam about 8 inches from sticks, lightly spray top of each and then dust with garlic powder and oregano.
4.   Bake at 375 degrees F about 20 to 25 minutes or until golden brown. Cool in pan on rack to serve within a day or two.

Olive Garden Caprese Salad

This classic tomato and mozzarella salad is perfect at the Olive Garden. Try this quick and easy copycat recipe in your own home and impress your guests with such a simple, yet flavorful dish.

Serves: 4

Ingredients

*   1 pound vine-ripened tomatoes, sliced .25 inch thick
*   1 ounce balsamic vinegar
*   1/4 cup basil, fresh
*   12 ounce whole milk or buffalo mozzarella
*   1 pinch oregano, dried
*   Salt, to taste
*   Fresh ground pepper, to taste
*   2 tablespoon extra-virgin olive oil

Instructions

1.   On a large platter, arrange sliced tomatoes and drizzle with balsamic vinegar.
2.   Place one basil leaf on top of each tomato slice.
3.   Slice mozzarella and place on top of basil leaves.
4.   Sprinkle oregano, salt and black pepper on cheese and drizzle with the olive oil.

Olive Garden Chicken Marsala

Learn how to make chicken marsala from one of the most popular restaurant chains in America. This delightful copycat recipe is easy to make and produces a delicious product every time.

Serves: 4

Ingredients

- 4 boneless, skinless chicken breast halves, pounded .25 inch thick
- 1/4 cup Wondra flour
- 1/2 teaspoon salt
- 1/8 teaspoon freshly ground black pepper
- 1/2 teaspoon oregano
- 4 tablespoon oil
- 4 tablespoon butter or margarine
- 1 cup fresh mushrooms, sliced
- 1/2 cup Marsala wine

Instructions

1. Combine flour, salt, pepper and oregano and blend well.

2. Heat the oil and butter in a skillet until bubbling lightly.

3. Dredge the chicken in the flour and shake off the excess. Cook the chicken on medium heat for about 2 minutes on the first side, until lightly brown. As you turn the breasts to the second side to cook, add the mushrooms around the chicken pieces. Cook about 2

more minutes, until lightly browned on the second side. Stir in the mushrooms. When the second side is lightly browned, add the wine around the pieces, cover the pan and simmer for about 10 minutes.

Olive Garden Fettuccine Alfredo

Fettuccine Alfredo is a classic Italian dish and a popular restaurant offering. Now you can recreate the Olive Garden's famous version with this restaurant copycat recipe.

Ingredients
- 1 pint heavy cream
- 1/2 cup butter
- 2 tablespoon cream cheese
- 3/4 cup Parmesan cheese
- 1 teaspoon garlic powder
- 8 ounce fettuccine, cooked and drained
- Salt and pepper, to taste

Instructions
1. In a saucepan combine butter, heavy cream, and cream cheese. Simmer this until all is melted, and mixed well. Add the Parmesan cheese and garlic powder. Simmer this for 15 - 20 minutes over low heat.
2. Toss pasta lightly with sauce, coating well. Leftovers freeze well.

Olive Garden House Dressing

The best part about dinner at the Olive Garden is the complimentary salad and bread sticks. Now you can recreate the delicious Italian dressing in your own home with this quick and easy copycat recipe.

Ingredients

- 8 ounce Paul Newman's Vinegar and Oil dressing

- 1/2 teaspoon basil, dried

- 1/2 teaspoon oregano, dried

- 3 packets of Sweet and Low or 1 tablespoon sugar

Instructions

1. Put ingredients into a bottle and shake well. Refrigerate 24 hours before using.

APPETIZER

Cause your home to feel like a café with these simple copycat canapés. Set aside some cash and make these hors d'oeuvres simply the manner in which you like them — with additional zest or without. Regardless of whether you're longing for Chinese, Italian, or great American, we have you secured.

Outback Steakhouse Gold Coast Coconut Shrimp

Menu Description: "Six monster shrimp plunged in lager player, abounded in coconut, southern style to a brilliant earthy colored and presented with preserves sauce."

The three organizers of Outback Steakhouse are an accomplished parcel of restaurateurs. Tim Gannon, Chris Sullivan, and Bob Basham had each worked for the Steak and Ale chain of cafés at once or another, just as other huge easygoing feasting chains. When the three got together to open a couple of cafés in the Tampa, Florida territory, they had unassuming desire.

Basham told Food and Beverage magazine, "We assumed if we split the benefits with what we figured we could make out of five or six cafés, we could have a pleasant lifestyle and play a great deal of golf." The initial six eateries opened inside 13 months. After eight years the chain had developed to more than 300 cafés, and the three men presently have a, pleasant lifestyle.

Coconut Shrimp is a sweet and fresh seared hors d'oeuvre not found on most different menus, particularly with the delectable jelly sauce. Outback servers guarantee it's a top vender.

At the café network, you get six of these shrimps to serve two as a tidbit, yet since we're setting aside the effort to make the player and utilize the entirety of that oil, I thought I'd up the respect twelve shrimp in this Outback Steakhouse coconut shrimp copycat recipe to serve four as a hors d'oeuvre. If you would prefer not to make that many, you can utilize a similar recipe with less shrimp and spare the extra hitter to make all the more later or simply pitch it.

Outback Steakhouse Bloomin Onion

Menu Description: "An Outback Ab-Original from Russell's Marina Bay."

If you go to an Outback Steakhouse expecting colorful Aussie grassland food that somebody like Crocodile Dundee would have appreciated, you're going to be somewhat frustrated, mate. With the exception of a little Australia-themed gear on the dividers, similar to boomerangs and pictures of kangaroos, the café network is about as "down under" as McDonald's is Scottish. The three authors, Tim Gannon, Chris Sullivan, and Bob Basham, are all U.S. young men. What's more, the menu, which is around 60 percent meat, contains chiefly American toll with charming Australian names like The Melbourne, Jackeroo Chops, and Chicken on the Barbie.

The organizers state they picked the Aussie topics because "Most Australians are carefree and gregarious individuals and easygoing individuals. We imagined that is actually the sort of benevolence and climate we need to have in our cafés."

In just six years, Outback Steakhouse has become the main steakhouse chain—to some degree because of the Bloomin' Onion: a huge, rotisserie onion cut to seem as though a blossom in sprout that was made by one of the eatery's organizers. What makes the starter so engaging other than its elegant appearance is the onion's fresh spiced covering, alongside the tasty plunging sauce, cunningly introduced in the focal point of the onion.

The café utilizes a unique gadget to make the cutting procedure simpler, yet you can make the entry points with a sharp knife. It just takes a consistent hand and a touch of care. This is the manner by which they did it in the beginning of the chain.

Bison Wild Wings Buffalo Wings and Sauces

Menu Description: "Here they are in the entirety of their lip-smacking, grant winning magnificence: Buffalo, New York-style chicken wings spun in your preferred mark sauce."

Since Buffalo, New York was excessively far away, Jim Disbrow and Scott Lowery fulfilled their mind-boggling needing in 1981 by opening a fiery chicken wing café near and dear in Kent, Ohio. With signature sauces and a happy environment, the chain has now developed from a school grounds sports bar with wings to a family eatery with more than 300 units. While fricasseeing chicken wings is no genuine mystery—just drop them in hot shortening for around 10 minutes—the heavenly fiery sauces make the wings uncommon. There are 12 assortments of sauce accessible to cover your firm chicken parts at the chain, and I'm introducing clones for the more conventional flavors. These sauces are exceptionally thick, practically like dressing or plunge, so we'll utilize an emulsifying method that will guarantee a rich last item where the oil won't discrete from different ingredients. Here is the chicken wing cooking and covering method, trailed by clones for the most well-known sauces: Spicy Garlic, Medium and Hot. The sauce recipes may appear to be identical from the outset, however every ha slight varieties make your sauce more sweltering or milder by altering the degree of cayenne pepper. You can discover Frank's pepper sauce by the other hot sauces in your market. If you can't find that brand, you can likewise utilize Crystal Louisiana hot sauce.

Margaritaville Volcano Nachos

Menu Description: "Bested with bean stew, cheddar, guacamole, sharp cream, jalapenos, tomato and scallions."

This mammoth heap of nachos satisfies its name and these are by a long shot the best nachos I have ever had at any easygoing chain. The mystery is in the stacking of the ingredients. You start with a layer of yellow corn tortilla chips and afterward spoon on some rich, marginally zesty nacho cheddar. I found that Tostitos makes the ideal cheddar for this: Tostitos Salsa Con Queso. More chips go on top, then more cheddar, then more chips followed by bean stew and a destroyed cheddar mix. Use premade bean stew that can often be found in the shop area of your market where the soups are sold. After the nachos are prepared and the cheddar is dissolved, diced tomato, green onion, harsh cream, guacamole and jalapeno cuts are included top, and the gathering would now be able to eject.

Margaritaville Jamaica Mistaica Wings

Menu Description: "Return to Jamaica! Our wings hurled in habanero-nectar wing sauce with cucumber sticks and house-made mango farm plunging sauce."

Chicken wings. Everybody adores the delightful non-working chicken parts. When they're acceptable, they're genuine acceptable. What's more, these little folks from

Jimmy Buffet's chain of island-themed cafés are probably the best. The arrangement is no large mystery: Fry the wings, include the sauce. It's that habanero nectar sauce recipe that makes these so great. Add to that a simple to-make mango farm plunging sauce and you're off on a relentless voyage to chicken wing heaven. The eatery serving size is for 10 wings, yet these top mystery ingredients will be sufficient for 30 wings.

Margaritaville Crab, Shrimp and Mushroom Dip

Menu Description: "Our mark appetizer...jumbo irregularity blue crab meat, bay shrimp and mushrooms, stewed in a Cajun cream sauce and presented with toasted garlic bread. We make it here so you know it's acceptable!"

This plunges shakes, and I'm by all account not the only one who thinks so. As indicated by the Margaritaville menu, it's the subject chain's mark starter. What's more, could you ask for anything better: scrumptious blue crab, minimal straight shrimp and cut mushrooms are largely swimming in a Cajun-style cream sauce, bested with liquefied Cheddar and Jack cheeses, and seared until the cheddar melts...yum. Present your clone with cuts of newly toasted rich garlic bread and you have an extraordinary gathering nibble. The café rendition is a little serving that is scarcely enough for two, so I've supersized this clone recipe to make enough plunge to fulfill The Brady Bunch.

LongHorn Steakhouse Firecracker Chicken Wraps

Menu Description: "Firm, seared flour tortillas loaded down with zesty flame broiled chicken and cheddar, presented with cool avocado-lime plunging sauce."

This Top Secret Recipes adaptation of the top of the line signature tidbit dish from the well known steakhouse chain will deliver a serving that is over multiple times greater than the plate you get at the café. That settles on this recipe the ideal decision for any major event get-together or bubbly occasion get-together where you've focused on turning into the occasion's finger food genius. You can make the envelops ahead of schedule by the day or even the day preceding and afterward fry them off at party time, however I would make the avocado-lime plunging sauce as near spending time in jail as conceivable since the avocado in the sauce will brown following several hours. I thought that it was generally advantageous to utilize a Cheddar and Monterey Jack cheddar mix which is anything but difficult to track down in many stores, however if your market doesn't have the mix just use ½ cup every one of the two destroyed cheeses.

Houlihan's Shrooms

Menu Description: "Large mushroom tops loaded up with herb and garlic cheddar, delicately battered and seared. Presented with fiery horseradish and mustard plunge made with Gray Poupon."

In a March 1986 story which ran in the Kansas City Times, a quarrel emitted between Gilbert/Robinson, the parent organization of Houlihan's café at that point, and two folks assembling their own chain of bars called Mike Houlihan's. The leader of the Houlihan's chain, Fred Hipp, said that from the start Houlihan's wouldn't fret so a lot, asking benevolent that the name not be utilized. In any case, when Mike Heyer and John Houlihan opened a Mike Houlihan's in St. Louis just a couple of squares from a unique Houlihan's café, Fred saw no decision however to sue. Before long, occupants with the family name were writing to Fred asking him to drop the claim. "You'll feel good, thirteen hundred Houlihans will beel better, and two Irishmen will have $50,000 to purchase progressively Irish bourbon," said one letter.

Here's another Houlihan's exemplary recipe called "Shrooms"— cheddar filled, player singed mushrooms served quite hot. You have the decision of making the herb-enhanced cheddar filling from the recipe here, or if you're feeling particularly lethargic, you can purchase a comparative premade filling. Be cautious when you first nibble into these fellows. Straight out of the fryer, the hot cheddar filling resembles liquid magma on your tongue and lips. Expend with care.

Joe's Stone Crab Jumbo Lump Crab Cakes

Joseph Weiss was living in New York with his wife and child when his primary care physician revealed to him he would require a difference in atmosphere to support his asthma. He traveled to Miami, Florida in 1913 and found he had the option to inhale once more. He immediately moved his family down South and opened his first café, a little lunch counter. Joe's café business detonated in 1921 when he found how to cook and serve the stone crabs got off the coast. Joe heated up the substantial hooks and served them chilled with a mystery mustard plunging sauce. Today just a single pincer is expelled from each stone crab, then the crab is hurled once again into the sea where it will recover the missing hook in around 2 years. The stone crabs, notwithstanding a few other mark things, made Joe's a Miami hotspot, and nowadays Joe's eateries can be found in Chicago and Las Vegas. Here is my interpretation of Joe's astounding mammoth crab cakes, which are produced using bump crab meat, and filled in as a starter or dish at the café. Obviously, you can't clone a Joe's crab dish without cloning the mystery mustard sauce, so recipe is here as well.

KFC Honey BBQ Wings

When an ordinary menu thing, these sweet, saucy wings are presently included to the KFC menu a "constrained time-in particular" premise in numerous business sectors. So how are we to get that clingy sauce all over our countenances and hands during those numerous months when we are pitilessly denied our

Honey BBQ Wings? Presently it's as simple as preparing this KFC nectar BBQ wings recipe that re-makes the firm breading on the chicken wings, and the sweet-and-smoky nectar BBQ sauce. "Constrained time-just" signs—we chuckle at you.

Houston's Chicago-Style Spinach Dip

Nowadays pretty much every easygoing eating chain has its rendition of this tidbit: spinach and artichoke hearts blended in with cheddar and flavors, presented hot with chips or saltines for plunging. Getting out and about throughout the years, I've attempted a considerable lot of them, and most recipes are almost indistinguishable. That is, with the exception of this one. Houston's makes their spinach plunge unique by utilizing a mix of harsh cream, Monterey Jack cheddar and Parmigiano Reggiano; a definitive Parmesan cheddar. Parmigiano Reggiano is conceived in Italy and is normally matured almost twice the length other, increasingly regular Parmesan cheeses. That fixing has the enormous effect in this plunge. So chase down a portion of this unique Parm at your all around loaded market or gourmet store, and you'll discover why Houston's spinach plunge has been one of the most mentioned recipe clones here at TSR.

KFC Cajun Honey Wings

These "Constrained Time Only" wings from KFC might be gone now, however since this clone copies the sweet-and-zesty sauce on this astonishing finger food, the incredible taste of this Dead Food lives on. In each store wings are covered with a KFC-style breading before they get seared up and hurled in delectable Cajun sauce. The sauce is a bomb on wings; however you can likewise give it something to do on ribs or other chicken parts like breaded tenders or prepared pieces. This recipe requires Emeril's Bayou Blast Cajun Seasoning, yet it will likewise work with some other Cajun flavoring mix you find in your nearby market.

Hooters Buffalo Shrimp

Menu Description: "It don't get any hitter than this."

With the two sided saying name and female servers (a significant number of whom are likewise models), Hooters has become an organization with pundits. Quite a while prior a gathering of Hooters Girls in Minneapolis sued the organization on grounds of sexual harassment, saying that the uniforms including shorts and tight T-shirts or tank tops were belittling. At last, the ladies dropped the suit. Be that as it may, all the more as of late, the Equal Employment Opportunity Commission requested the organization to recruit men on the foodservice staff. Hooters countered with a snide million-dollar promoting effort including a mustachioed man named "Vince" wearing Hooters Girl getup. By and by, that suit was dropped.

VP of Marketing, Mike McNeil disclosed to Nation's Restaurant News, "Hooter's Girls are really wearing more apparel than what most ladies wear at the exercise center or the sea shore. It's a piece of the idea. I don't figure the world would be a superior spot if we had folks be Hooters Girls." You may concur or deviate, yet the truth of the matter is that Hooters is presently the nation's thirteenth biggest supper house chain and one of the quickest developing, with an expanding number of coffee shops finding Buffalo Shrimp, a scrumptious side project of Buffalo Chicken Wings.

Hooters Buffalo Shrimp Low-Fat

The Hooters chain proceeds with its quick development over the globe into 39 states and seven nations, including Taiwan, Aruba, Singapore, and Australia. In those 200 or so cafés, this starter has gotten extremely well known since it was first presented in 1995, as a minor departure from the Buffalo Chicken Wings recipe. Since this shrimp is seared, similar to the chicken wings, we should depend on certain stunts that will help cut the fat down. We'll heat the shrimp, as opposed to sear it, and set up the sauce with a sans fat spread that includes flavor.

Olive Garden Stuffed Mushrooms

Menu Description: "Parmesan, Romano and mozzarella cheddar, shellfishes and herb breadcrumbs prepared in mushroom tops."

Breadcrumbs, shellfishes and three sorts of cheddar are heated into white mushroom tops in this clone of a top pick from Olive Garden's hors d'oeuvre menu. Combine all the stuffing ingredients in a bowl, fill the mushroom tops, sprinkle on some minced red ringer pepper, spread the mushrooms with a cover of mozzarella cheddar cuts, and prepare. Following 15 minutes you'll have an incredible canapé or hors d'oeuvre for 4 to 6 individuals—that is double the serving size of the dish from the eatery.

P.F. Chang's Vegetarian Lettuce Wraps

Menu Description: "Wok-burned tofu, red onions, water chestnuts with mint and lime. Presented with cool lettuce cups."

In the wake of distributing the first form of my clone for this current chain's Chicken in Soothing Lettuce Wraps in 2006 I started getting demands for a clone of the veggie lover rendition. I was reluctant to try and attempt the veggie lover form believing that it couldn't in any way, shape or form be as heavenly as the chicken variant. Kid, was I wrong. The red onion, lime squeeze and mint set these lettuce wraps separated, and finely diced prepared tofu replaces the chicken. Prepared tofu has a dull outside and is a lot firmer than ordinary tofu. If you can't discover it at your grocery store you can get it at Asian markets or in claim to fame stores, for example, Whole Foods. It arrives in an assortment of flavors like teriyaki and curry; however you need the unflavored stuff. Cut it by cutting it into flimsy cuts, cut those cuts down the middle the long way, and afterward cutting over those julienned cuts so you end up with extremely little diced pieces. Wrench your oven up as high as it goes for this one.

On the Border Guacamole Live!

Menu Description: "Specially made new, with ready avocados and selection of tomatoes, jalapenos, cilantro, red onions and new lime juice. Enough to share."

This 160-unit easygoing Mexican chain makes a decent tableside guacamole that you can without much of a stretch copy for your amigos. This is the essential equation; however you can unreservedly modify it to suit the flavors of your group. It's likewise simple to twofold it (or more) for a greater celebration, if that is the arrangement. You might need to place the avocados into the refrigerator for an hour or two preceding you open them up. This Guac is greatly improved when marginally chilled.

Olive Garden Smoked Mozzarella Fonduta

Menu Description: "Broiler prepared smoked mozzarella, provolone, Parmesan and Romano cheddar. Presented with Tuscan bread."

Olive Garden's interpretation of the Italian softened cheddar plunge incorporates smoked mozzarella joined with ground Parmesan, Romano, and provolone cheddar, and loads of thyme. When causing your clone, to make certain to cut the waxy skin off the smoked mozzarella before you grind it. That part doesn't taste great. After gradually softening the mozzarella, Parmesan, and Romano in a little pan with creamer, empty the rich blend into a shallow dish, top it with a cut of provolone, and pop it under the grill until light earthy colored. Serve your hot fonduta with loaf cuts, bagel chips, or saltines.

Applebee's Pizza Sticks

Menu Description: "Parmesan: Thin dried up pieces of pizza batter beat with herbs and softened Italian cheddar, presented with marinara sauce. Stacked: Add Italian frankfurter and pepperoni."

Each Applebee's puts forth an attempt to embellish within the eatery with pictures and memorabilia from the area in which it is found. You'll see photos of nearby legends and understudies, tags, standards, old gifts, knickknacks, and collectibles all speaking to region history. Investigate the dividers of the following Applebee's you visit. Perhaps you can discover something you lost quite a long while prior.

In the interim, here's a discover: pizza sticks that are produced using mixture that is sealed, singed, and afterward cooked. The broiling includes a remarkable flavor and surface to the mixture that you won't get with conventional pizza. I've structured this present Applebee's pizza sticks copycat recipe to utilize the premade batter that comes in tubes. You know, similar to the stuff from that mixture kid. In any case, you can make this with any batter recipe you like. Simply fold the mixture into a 10x15-inch square shape before cutting.

These hors d'oeuvres can be made either in the Parmesan rendition without meat, or "stacked" with hotdog and pepperoni. This recipe yields a ton, so it makes great gathering food.

Applebee's Baja Potato Boats Reduced-Fat

This is Applebee's minor departure from the mainstream potato skins tidbit put on the map by T.G.I. Friday's. Many appear to lean toward these to customary potato skins because of their south-of-the-outskirt style. The main issue is a serving has around 12 grams of fat (much more if you thud on some harsh cream). Also, that is for just three pieces. If you for the most part don't stop there, you may be keen on this TSR adaptation of the delectable dish, which eliminates the excess by 66 percent. Presently you can eat three fold the amount of these Mexican-style potato skin wedges for a similar measure of fat as the genuine article, on account of diminished fat cheddar and sans fat harsh cream.

Bonefish Grill Saucy Shrimp

Menu Description: "Wild inlet shrimp sauteed in a Lime Tomato Garlic sauce with Kalamata olives and Feta cheddar."

Restaurateurs Tim Curci and Chris Parker opened the main Bonefish Grill in St. Petersburg, Florida in 2000, and, with at any rate eight types of new oak-flame broiled fish to browse on some random day, the chain has since detonated to more than 100 units in 24 states. Truly, the fish is generally excellent, and the oak barbecue is a pleasant touch, however you ought to likewise realize this is a café that likes to play around with sauces. This starter clone is a genuine case of that. The pungency of the lime works beautifully with the pleasantness of the sundried tomato to make a scampi sauce not at all like any you may have tasted previously. Lay this basic dish on the soldiers before your principle course and you will be today around evening time's kitchen saint.

California Pizza Kitchen Tuscan Hummus

Menu Description: "Our unique recipe of Tuscan white beans pureed with sesame, garlic, lemon, and flavors. Decorated with new Roma tomatoes, basil, and garlic. Presented with warm pizza-pita bread."

The customary dish of Tuscan white beans is typically produced using dried cannellini beans or extraordinary Northern beans that are absorbed for the time being water and afterward cooked until delicate with olive oil, garlic and sage. Be that as it may, there's no compelling reason to hold up through such a tedious procedure if we can essentially utilize effectively delicate canned beans found in any market. Search for white beans or the somewhat bigger extraordinary Northern beans and strain off the fluid, however don't discard that fluid! you'll require a tad bit of it to add to the food processor alongside different ingredients, including sesame tahini which can be found in many markets where the universal nourishments are loaded or in strength stores, for example, Whole Foods.

Applebee's Mozzarella Sticks Low-Fat/Low-Calorie

I initially made this recipe for an appearance on The Dr. Oz Show in a fragment about more advantageous clone forms of famous café tidbits (watch it here). However, with two different recipes to demo the section was excessively fat and this one got cut. Along these lines, I've stopped the recipe here on the site for you to utilize. This recipe copies the flavor of Applebee's Mozzarella Sticks however the fat and calories are cut significantly by preparing the sticks as opposed to utilizing the customary searing technique. Set up these early since the sticks need to sit for in any event 2 hours in your cooler before you prepare them.

Bonefish Grill Bang Shrimp

Menu Description: "Delicate, firm wild bay shrimp hurled in a rich, zesty sauce."

Bonefish Grill gladly alludes to this tidbit as the "house claim to fame." And why not, it's an alluring dish with beat up flavor, particularly if you like your food on the zesty side. The warmth in this Bang Shrimp recipe originates from the mystery ingredient mix that is enhanced with bean stew garlic sauce, otherwise called sambal. You can locate this brilliant red sauce where the Asian nourishments in your market—and keeping in mind that you're there, get some rice vinegar. When the sauce is made, you coat the shrimp in a basic prepared breading, fry them to a pleasant brilliant earthy colored, hurl them delicately in the sauce, and afterward serve them up on a bed of blended greens to hungry people who, ideally, have a cool beverage close by to smooth the sting.

BJ's Restaurant and Brew house Avocado Egg Rolls

Menu Description: "Firm brilliant wontons wrap an enticing mix of avocados, cream cheddar, sun-dried tomatoes, red onions, cilantro, pine nuts, chipotle peppers and flavors. Presented with a sweet tamarind sauce."

Avocado egg rolls or spring moves appear to be expanding in fame as a tidbit at easygoing chains, however they are more of a high support menu thing than, state, southwestern egg rolls, or other spring move varieties. Since avocados rush to oxidize and turn earthy colored, these rolls must be made and served inside a 2 to 12 hour time span. Additionally, cooks must be mindful so as not to over fry the egg rolls or the avocado inside will turn out to be excessively hot, turn earthy colored, and taste quite gross. Thus, if you're intending to serve these later in the day, make them toward the beginning of the day and let them relax in your refrigerator until it's an ideal opportunity to cook them. You can likewise make the tamarind sauce promptly in the day and park it in the ice chest. You'll require a little tamarind glue for this sauce, which can be found at Whole Foods or claim to fame stores. If you would prefer not to clone the sauce as served in the café, you can generally utilize your preferred sweet and additionally hot packaged plunging sauces. Rich southwestern-style plunging sauces are additionally amazing on these.

T.G.I. Friday's Potato Skins Reduced-Fat

Potato skins are beneficial for you, yet those at chain eateries can be stacked with fat and calories. For my appearance on The Dr. Oz Show I made this rendition utilizing oil shower, turkey bacon and diminished fat cheddar to clone the celebrated potato skins, yet with around 33% of the calories and one-fourth of the fat.

Planet Hollywood Pizza Bread

Menu Description: "New prepared on premises, cut into eight pieces, brushed with garlic spread, Parmesan cheddar, mozzarella and basil, beat with cleaved plum tomatoes and herbed olive oil."

In 1988, London-conceived eatery big shot Robert Ian Earl got together with film maker Keith Barrish and a gaggle of big names including Arnold Schwarzenegger, Sylvester Stallone, Bruce Willis, and Demi Moore to begin a Hollywood-themed café that is en route to turning into his best endeavor yet. In 1991, a function ritzy undertaking in New York City commended the opening of the world's first Planet Hollywood.

Be that as it may, even the coolest topic café won't fly if the food doesn't please. Baron disclosed to Nation's Restaurant News, "Individuals don't eat subjects—no idea on the planet can prevail for long except if it additionally conveys incredible food at the correct value." Planet Hollywood highlights a menu of delightful dishes equaling food from mainstream stores that don't have a topic to incline toward.

The Pizza Bread hors d'oeuvre comes energetically suggested via Planet Hollywood servers. The "bread" is pizza batter, moved dainty, with a light layer of cheddar, basil and tomato on top; then it's heated in a pizza stove at the eatery. Since the majority of us don't have pizza broilers at home, this recipe has been intended for a regular gas or electric stove.

Roadhouse Grill Roadhouse Cheese Wraps

Menu Description: "Our unique 'eggrolls' loaded down with Cheddar and Monterey Jack cheddar, green onions and a bit of jalapeno peppers. Presented with marinara."

This minor departure from the well-known seared cheddar sticks hors d'oeuvre disguises zesty jalapeno peppers and green onions in the center, and it's totally enveloped with huge spring move wrapper before singing. The marinara sauce as an afterthought is ideal for plunging the gooey goody, yet you may likewise attempt your preferred salsa. To spare time—and we as a whole like that—utilization your most loved packaged marinara sauce for plunging so you won't have to prepare some without any preparation.

Simon Kitchen and Bar Wok-Charred Edamame

In 2008 Chef Kerry Simon got together his blades at the Hard Rock Casino and Hotel and moved over the Las Vegas Strip into the Palms Place tower at the Palms. The new eatery includes a portion of a similar solace food top choices as the old joint, for example, truffled and cheddar and cotton candy for dessert, however Kerry has now included a sushi bar and a more extensive menu which incorporates breakfast, lunch and an unquestionable requirement attempt Sunday informal breakfast where you might be eating close by any semblance of Avril Lavigne or Hugh Hefner and his sweethearts. When you're noodling over which hors d'oeuvres to attempt you should look at this heavenly irresistible edamame starter: A heap of soybeans are cooked over high warmth in a wok until their cases are darkened in spots, then they're hurled in new lime juice and a Japanese 7-flavor flavoring called shichimi togarashi. Togarashi is a zesty mix of orange strip, sesame seeds, kelp and bean stew that you can buy in most Asian markets or on the web. The mix for the most part does exclude salt, so you'll need to include a portion of that too before you delve in. Or then again, you can utilize Szechwan flavoring, for example, one made by Sun-Bird that is found in most supermarkets where the Asian nourishments are stopped. These mixes will for the most part have salt in them, so you presumably don't have to include extra salt if you utilize the Szechwan flavoring. You'll need to cook these in a wok that has been preheated over a fire on a gas oven, or you can utilize a cast-iron skillet that has been preheated for in any event 10 minutes - you should see a great deal of smoke when you drop those beans in the container! Turn on the vent over your oven before you begin cooking except if you have to test your smoke alarms.

Red Lobster Scallops And Bacon

At the time I was composing this book there were two different ways you could have your bacon and scallops at Red Lobster: wrapped and seared, or barbecued on a stick. The previous is a littler segment to be filled in as a starter, while the flame broiled adaptation is filled in as a fundamental course. I've included recipes to clone the two adaptations.

Ruby Tuesday Queso Dip

Menu Description: "Smooth and zesty cheddar plunge. Presented with boundless fresh tortilla chips."

Numerous who have attempted the first state it's the best queso plunge they've at any point had, so I needed to jump looking into the issue. Conversing with a head supervisor I discovered that the plunge is made with American cheddar and a little Parmesan, however the remainder of the ingredients would need to be resolved in the underground lab. When I got down there— utilizing the lift covered up in a phony latrine toward the side of an empty parcel—I promptly washed the plunge in a sifter and found bits of spinach, onion and two sorts of peppers. The red pepper, which is answerable for the kick, had all the earmarks of being rehydrated dry peppers. It would seem that they're red jalapenos, yet since the red ones can be elusive I slashed up some red Fresno peppers and the plunge tasted extraordinary— brimming with flavor with a pleasant fiery kick. Simply make certain to evacuate the inward films and seeds from the peppers before you mince them up, or your cool plunge may wind up pressing a ton of warmth.

Ruby Tuesday Thai Phoon Shrimp

Menu Description: "Delicate, firm shrimp with a sweet and hot stew sauce that is got the perfect kick."

This was another activity for the smaller scale screen strainer. Washing endlessly the mayo from a spoonful of this delectable bean stew sauce uncovers exactly what I expected: sambal pieces. The minced bean stew peppers that stayed there, presently bare, in the base of the strainer, looked simply like the sort of red pepper utilized in sambal bean stew sauce. Also, since there were bits of garlic in there as well, unmistakably the splendid red stew garlic sauce you find close to the Asian nourishments in your market is the ideal mystery element for the red hot blend that is utilized on this famous dish from Ruby Tuesday's hors d'oeuvre menu. When you make the sauce, prepare a portion of the mystery breading for the shrimp and continue ahead with the browning. You can utilize shortening or oil here, however I think shortening works best, and it doesn't smell up the house. The no trans-fat stuff is da bomb. When the entirety of your shrimps are seared to a pleasant brilliant earthy colored, cautiously cover the little suckers with about portion of the sauce, and afterward serve the remainder of the sauce as an afterthought for plunging, much the same as they do at the café.

T.G.I. Friday's Nine-Layer Dip

Menu Description: "Refried beans, cheddar, guacamole, dark olives, prepared acrid cream, green onions, tomatoes and cilantro. Presented with tortilla chips and new salsa."

When the first T.G.I. Friday's opened in New York City in 1965 as a gathering place for single grown-ups, Newsweek and The Saturday Evening Post detailed that it was the start of the "singles age." Today the café's clients have developed, many are hitched, and they carry their kids with them to the in excess of 300 Friday's the nation over and around the globe.

The Nine-Layer Dip is an often mentioned starter on the T.G.I. Friday's menu. This dish will serve about six individuals effectively, so it's ideal for a little assembling. Try not to stress if there's just two or three you—extras can be refrigerated for a day or two.

T.G.I. Friday's Potato Skins

Menu Description: "Stacked with cheddar and bacon. Presented with sharp cream and chives."

Scent sales rep Alan Stillman was a solitary person in New York City in 1965, searching for an approach to meet ladies who lived in his neighborhood. He made sense of an approach to stand out enough to be noticed: purchase a separated lager joint in the zone, jazz it up, and call it "The T.G.I.F." to pull in the profession swarm. Inside seven days, police had blockaded the region to control swarms running to Alan's new café. The eatery made $1 million in its first year—a great deal of mixture in those days. Before long restaurateurs the nation over were mimicking the idea.

In 1974 T.G.I. Friday's imagined a hors d'oeuvre that would likewise be replicated by numerous individuals in the next years. Potato skins are as yet the most well-known thing on the T.G.I. Friday's menu, with about 4 million requests served each year. The recipe has the additional advantage of giving you extra prepared potato prepared for crushing.

T.G.I. Friday's Parmesan-Crusted Sicilian Quesadilla

Menu Description: "Our flour tortilla is pressed with sauteed chicken, hotdog, bruschetta marinara, bacon and overflowing with Monterey Jack cheddar. We cover it with Parmesan, and sear it to a firm, brilliant earthy colored, then sprinkle it with balsamic coating."

Italy meets Mexico in this new hit tidbit that consolidates a cheddar filled tortilla with ingredients you wouldn't as a rule find inside a quesadilla, including Friday's bruschetta marinara. Parmesan cheddar is crusted outwardly of the tortilla, and the balsamic coating sprinkle is the ideal completing touch. This is a wonderful gathering dish canapé since the entire recipe makes 4 quesadillas that can each be cut into upwards of 8 pieces.

Cheesecake Factory Bruschetta

Menu Description: "Flame broiled Bread Topped with Fresh Chopped Tomato, Red Onion, Garlic, Basil and Olive Oil."

In 1972, Oscar and Evelyn Overton moved from Detroit to Los Angeles to construct a discount pastry shop that would offer cheesecakes and other great pastries to neighborhood eateries. Business was a blasting achievement, however a few cafés scoffed at the significant expenses the bread shop was charging for its pastries. Along these lines, in 1978, the couple's child David chose to open his very own eatery—the main Cheesecake Factory café—in elegant Beverly Hills. The eatery was a prompt achievement and soon David began an extension of the idea. Without a doubt, the present aggregate of 20 cafés doesn't appear to be a great deal, yet his bunch of stores procures the chain more than $100 million in business every year. That is more than certain chains with multiple times the quantity of outlets rake in.

Bruschetta is one of the top-selling tidbits at the café network. Bruschetta is toasted bread enhanced with garlic and olive oil, cooked until firm, and afterward orchestrated around a heap of tomato-basil serving of mixed greens in vinaigrette. This plate of mixed greens is scooped onto the bruschetta, and afterward you open wide. This adaptation makes five cuts simply like the dish served at the café, yet the recipe can be effortlessly multiplied.

Hooters Buffalo Chicken Wings Reduced-Fat

You likely needn't bother with me to disclose to you that conventional chicken wings have significant fat and calories. As a rule, the wings are pan fried in hot oil, the skin is left on the chicken, and afterward they are covered in a fiery sauce that is as a rule around half spread. Great stuff without a doubt, yet in some cases you should enjoy a reprieve from the fat. So then, how might we diminish the fat in a clone recipe for what has gotten one of the most mainstream chicken wings around without bargaining the flavor and everything else that makes the Hooters form so incredible?

As a matter of first importance, we should sear and prepare them as opposed to utilizing the conventional fricasseeing strategy. As the wings sear we keep the skin on so the meat won't dry out. When the wings have cooled a bit, we remove the skin and supplant it with a prepared breading and a light covering of cooking splash. We prepare the wings until they're brilliant earthy colored, cover them with a hot wing sauce that is made with a light margarine seasoned spread instead of margarine, and, presto—a Hooters Buffalo Chicken Wing clone that tips the scales at around 33% the fat of the first form.

T.G.I. Friday's BBQ Chicken Wings Reduced-Fat
You must hand it to him. Alan Stillman believed that if he opened his own eatery, it may be an extraordinary method to meet the airline stewards who lived in his New York City neighborhood. Not exclusively did the

buddy finish on his arrangement in 1965 with the first T.G.I. Friday's, however today the organization is 387 units solid.

Friday's kitchen thought of a scrumptious mix of grill sauce and creamy fruit spread for covering the southern style chicken wings. For our decreased fat clone, we'll re-make a similar taste of the grill sauce, yet we'll take the skin from the chicken wings and heat the wings to eliminate the excess route down.

Red Lobster Cheddar Bay Crab Bake

Counts on the prominence of the chain's Cheddar Bay Biscuits, Red Lobster gourmet experts made this pizza-molded tidbit with an outside layer produced using the scone mixture, and crab and cheddar prepared on top. If you like those delicate, mushy garlic rolls that accompany each feast at Red Lobster—and you like crab—then you'll certainly like this.

Hooters Original Style Wings

Menu Description: "The all in all! The style we developed more than 30 years prior; they're breaded by hand hurled in your decision of wing sauce and served by your preferred Hooters young lady."

When I previously hacked this recipe in 1997 for the book Top Secret Restaurant Recipes, Hooters wings appeared to be unique than they do today. The chain used to leave the pointy end of the wing joined to the center piece, or "level," which, in all honesty, is superfluous because there is next to no meat on the tip portion. Today the chain serves wings like every other person, with drumettes and pads totally isolated, and conveyed by servers in indistinguishable brilliant orange shorts from when the chain began in 1983.

One thing that wasn't accessible to me in those days was the chance to analyze the chain's bundling for the arrangements of ingredients on signature things like sauces and breading. Today, since they sell these things as retail items, I can exploit naming laws that expect ingredients to be plainly recorded and see what truly goes into these recipes. Utilizing that new data, I've made a couple of little changes to improve my recipe from more than 20 years back, including two forms of the kickass wing sauce—medium and hot—for your wing-eating up joy.

Cheesecake Factory Pork Belly Sliders

This heavenly new hors d'oeuvre from the Cheesecake Factory highlights four little sandwiches, each pressing enormous flavor. Smoked pork stomach is slathered with grill sauce, then stacked on delicate slider buns with fiery sauce, rich coleslaw, and fresh seared pickles. Smoked pork midsection is simply the star, so you'll either smoke some yourself utilizing a smoker or utilize your barbecue with the strategy portrayed in the Tidbits underneath. You need around 10 ounces of pork paunch to get 6 ounces when smoked, or 1½ ounces per sandwich.

The coleslaw is simple, the zesty sauce is simple, the grill sauce is premade (packaged), and the singed pickles are a straightforward exercise in breading and searing that anybody can ace. After the pork midsection is entirely smoked and self-destruct delicate, stack everything on your preferred toasted delicate slider rolls and let the eating up start.

Hooters Daytona Beach Style Wings

Hooters appeared another flavor and style of their renowned chicken wings in 2013 with the presentation of Daytona Beach Style Wings—exposed wings (not breaded) that are singed, sauced, and flame broiled. The new menu thing was a business achievement, overshadowing the renowned bison style wings the chain had gotten known for, and causing it basic that we to have a flavorful and precise copycat hack. What's more, presently we do.

To assemble an indistinguishable home form you'll first need to make a knockoff of the flavorful Daytona sauce to brush over the wings. It's a mix of grill sauce and a similar cayenne sauce used to cover customary bison wings, in addition to a couple of other significant ingredients that make the sauce uncommon—and things you won't find in different hacks—like Worcestershire sauce and minced jalapeños. The wings are covered, barbecued for one moment on each side, and then sauced again for most extreme flavor. Stack the napkins close by and get something tall to drink, because these muddled wings are ensured to convey a super-fiery kick to your food opening.

Cheesecake Factory Cheeseburger Spring Rolls

Here's the manner by which to manufacture a cheeseburger in fresh spring move mixture and make the mystery 4-fixing plunging sauce for an ideal hack of one of Cheesecake Factory's most current canapés. I found the best answer for a decent clone was to initially cook two 4-ounce Angus patties—with no under 15 percent fat so the meat remains delicious—in a sauté container until caramelized. I then sauteed some onion in a similar skillet and blended it into the disintegrated patties, with ketchup and diced American cheddar.

I attempted a few different wrappers and found the most slender wrappers to work the best. Attempt to discover wrappers that state "very meager" on them. Thicker mixture wrappers will rankle when singed, which isn't the means by which the café variant looks, despite the fact that the thicker wrappers despite everything make delectable spring rolls.

Rice paper wrappers will give you a chewier, less fresh chomp, and are a decent choice if you're keen on a sans gluten rendition. If you go with rice paper, you won't need the cornstarch answer for seal them. Dunking the entire wrapper in a little water makes the rice paper malleable and normally clingy.

Cheddar's Santa Fe Spinach Dip

Spinach plunges are an incredible finger food hors d'oeuvre and pretty much every chain has its own variant, yet Cheddar's has truly outstanding in the business with an exceptional, marginally fiery southwestern curve. Four different sorts of cheddar are utilized in this recipe: three are mixed into the spinach, and then mozzarella is liquefied over the top not long before serving.

Furthermore, for speed, we'll utilize a microwave to rapidly defrost the crate of solidified spinach with the goal that you'll have a delish spinach dunk on the table in only 20 minutes.

KFC Extra Crispy Tenders

As you can likely speculation, KFC's Extra Crispy Tenders are chicken tenderloins covered with a similar heavenly breading as KFC's Extra Crispy Chicken. These tenders come in servings of two, three, six, or twelve, with your decision of plunging sauces as an afterthought including wild ox, grill, and the new Finger Lickin' Good Sauce.

To copy these chicken strips at home we'll depend on a comparative prep method to the one utilized for the Extra Crispy Chicken: the chicken is tenderized for 2 hours to give it more flavor and succulence, then the tenders are twofold breaded for an extra-crunchy covering.

A significant mystery uncovered in this breading recipe is the utilization of a specific sort of ground dark pepper. For the best clone you need to utilize Tellicherry dark pepper, which is premium dark pepper ground from develop peppercorns that have had the opportunity to grow more flavor. The exceptional delayed flavor impression of KFC chicken is ascribed to this uncommon zest, so it merits an opportunity to follow it down.

Tellicherry dark pepper costs somewhat more than the more youthful, increasingly regular dark pepper, yet if you need a decent clone of the renowned firm singed chicken, it's a basic fixing. Make certain to granulate the pepper fine before including it.

California Pizza Kitchen Spicy Buffalo Cauliflower

Fresh cauliflower starters are rich at the chains nowadays, and not every one of them are adequate to be clone-commendable, yet CPK's interpretation of breaded cauliflower in wild ox wing sauce is a standout amongst other I've had. The fresh florets are made without gluten with rice flour and they are beautifully introduced in a puddle of farm dressing, sprinkled with Gorgonzola cheddar, and beat with julienned celery and green onions.

For the sauce, CPK culinary specialists join the kind of customary bison wings with sriracha and afterward improve it a piece. After a couple of attempts, I thought of a hack that is incredibly simple, requiring just four ingredients.

The player is much simpler, with just three ingredients—rice flour, buttermilk, and salt—and once your oil is sufficiently hot, it takes under 3 minutes to cook the cauliflower to flawlessness. After a delicate hurl in the mystery ingredient, you're prepared to plate your popular, tempting tidbit.

Wingstop Garlic Parmesan Wings

If you want to plunge into a heap of wings with huge flavor and no warmth, you'll love this hack of a top pick at Wingstop. At the café, these wings are flavorfully splashed with a rich garlic Parmesan season and afterward sprinkled with ground Parmesan cheddar. A home clone is simple by hurling fresh wings in this hack of the top mystery season, and garnish them with a snowfall of good Parmesan cheddar.

To copy the treat, you clarify a stick of margarine, then include a little oil with the goal that the spread doesn't solidify. Parmesan cheddar, garlic, and salt are blended in, then the sauce is put aside to cool and thicken.

When the wings are seared to a brilliant earthy colored, hurl them with the season in a bowl, then snatch the ground Parm and make it day off.

CONCLUSION

Thanks for taking this guide. I hope you have learnt a lot. It is essential to do as per the interest of this book for maximum efficiency.

Copycat recipes for mainstream eatery nourishments are all over. Truly, their authenticity can't be verified — corporate recipes are often held safely secured — yet your taste buds comprehend what's up, and a few recipes come near the firsts.

Needing Macintosh and cheddar from Panera's Bread or Panda Express' chow mein? What about Olive Garden's mark Italian plate of mixed greens dressing, or singed frozen yogurt like you find at your preferred Mexican home base?

There are a lot of copycat recipes for each of those, and, fortunately, they're not confused. Truth be told, they all can be made with things you either as of now have or most likely purchased a week ago when you alarm looked for bathroom tissue.

You know what your identity is.

And keeping in mind that we're grinding away, we should give proper respect to those ballpark and arena franks we're not eating at any game, anyplace, at any point in the near future.

CPSIA information can be obtained
at www.ICGtesting.com
Printed in the USA
LVHW051014161020
668886LV00007B/138